JEWEL ON THE YUKON

EAGLE CITY

Illustrated

Elva Scott
Eagle Historical Society & Museums
Eagle City, Alaska
March 1997

Library of Congress Cataloging-in-Publication Data

Scott, Elva R.

Jewel on the Yukon:
Eagle City

Collection of Essays
Bibliography
Illustrated

1. Alaska-Eagle City-description & history 2. Eagle City,
Alaska. 3. Yukon River-Alaska 4. Fortymile River-Alaska
5. Seventymile River-Alaska 6. Historic Eagle
and its People I. Title

1997 979.803

ISBN 0-9657188-0-8

Printed in the United States of America

Cover photo: Eagle City, Yukon River, Eagle bluff.
1948 by Frank Barr, pilot, photographer.
Photo courtesy: Nellie Briggs, Eagle Historical Society

JEWEL ON THE YUKON
EAGLE CITY

TABLE OF CONTENTS

This book is dedicated to the adventuresome spirit of the founders and early residents of beautiful Eagle City, so their stories of optimism, courage, hardships and pleasures may be preserved. Whether working on the creeks or living in town, they shared their good and bad times. Many, without relatives in the north, became a cohesive family, always ready to help others with their labor, materials and/or emotional support. What role models they became!

Special thanks to the old timer's relatives and friends for sharing the stories which had been recorded through diaries, letters, books and photographs. Esther and Anton Merly deserve special credit for recognizing the importance of these documents and saving the materials which have become the basis for the outstanding archives of the Eagle Historical Society and Museums.

Elva R. Scott
Eagle City, Alaska
March 1997

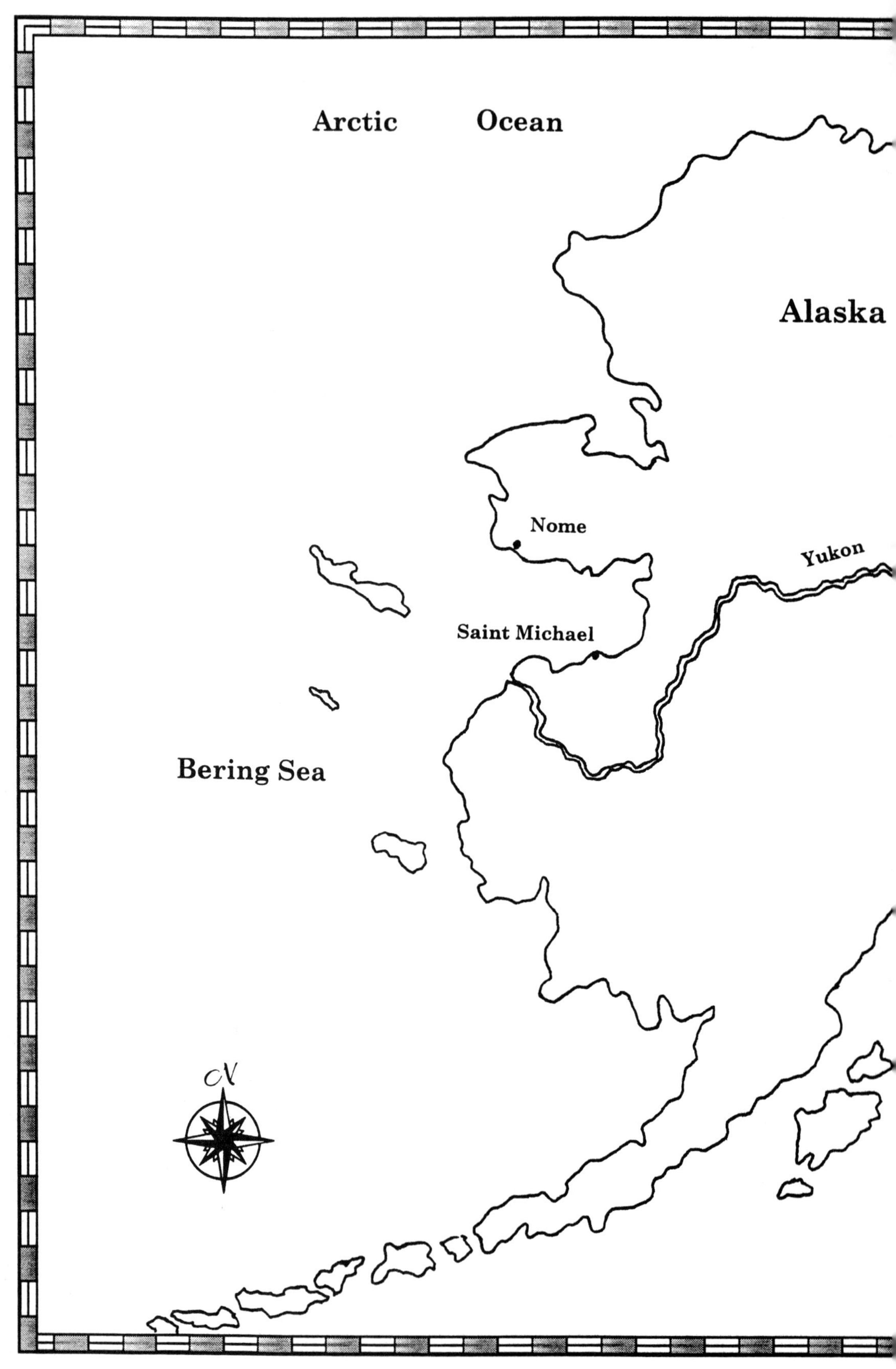

Arctic Ocean
Alaska
Nome
Yukon
Saint Michael
Bering Sea
N

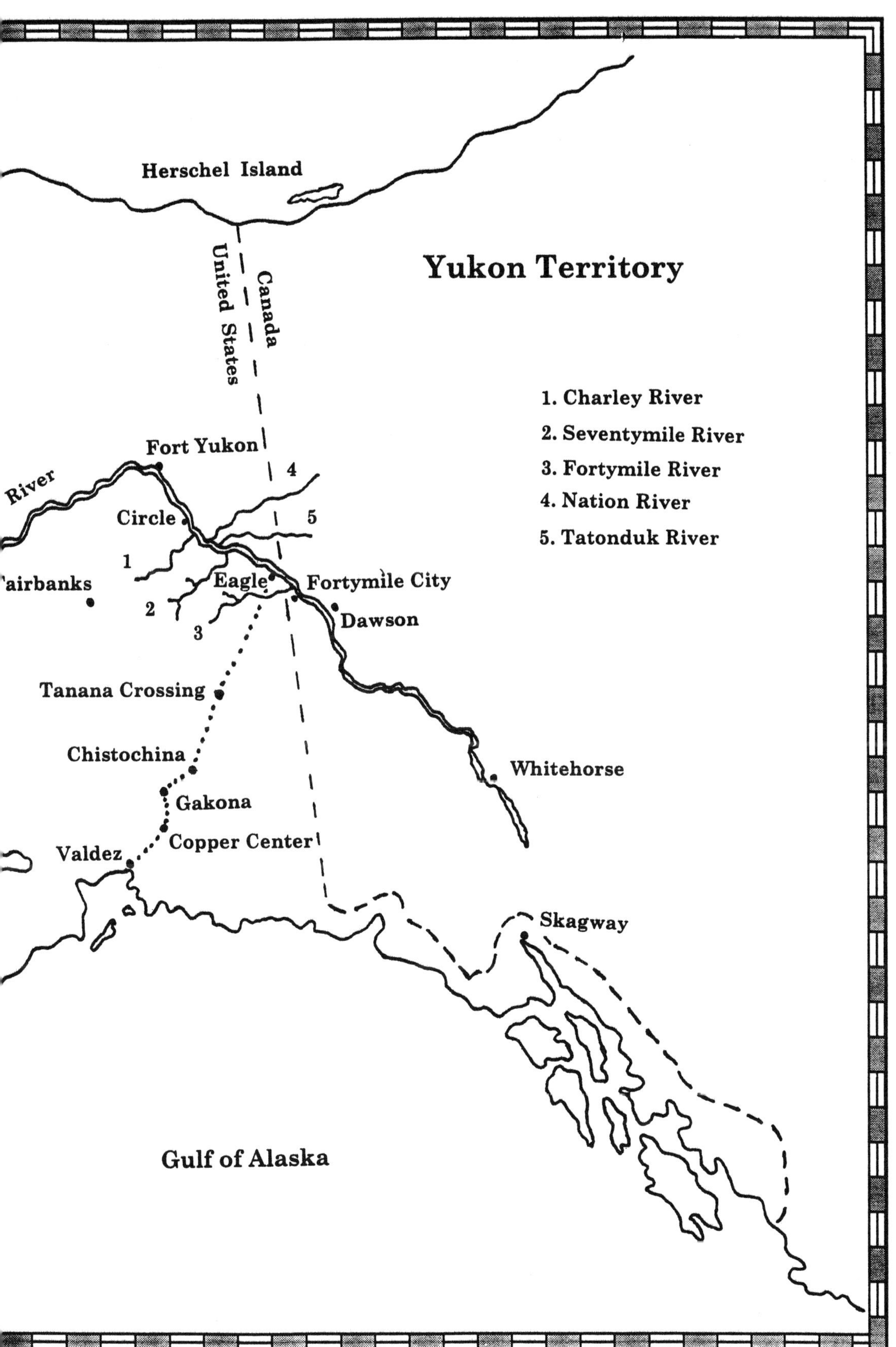

Herschel Island
Yukon Territory
Canada
United States
1. Charley River
2. Seventymile River
3. Fortymile River
4. Nation River
5. Tatonduk River
River
Fort Yukon
Circle
Fairbanks
Eagle
Fortymile City
Dawson
Tanana Crossing
Chistochina
Gakona
Copper Center
Valdez
Whitehorse
Skagway
Gulf of Alaska

CHAPTER I

EAGLE CITY
Overview

As the early settlers penetrated the vast interior of Alaska, they established their first communities on the banks of the rivers. In 1897 this was the case at Eagle City, which became the only planned gold rush town of that era. It had a colorful beginning as told by Cash Darrell (Darrell, 1946)

> *Eagle City was first conceived by a disgruntled Dawson stampeder whose name was Old Man Martin. He was under forty when he was afflicted with the urge to create a new Golconda. His idea was nourished by what he considered a great injustice upon the part of Colonel Steele and his red-coated minions.*
>
> *Martin had committed a minor infraction which was against the peace and dignity of the crown. "Three months on the woodpile," sternly sentenced the Court. This Royal brand of justice curdled the few remaining globules of respect Martin had for royalty.*
>
> *Martin gingerly rubbed his chafed wrists that still bore the degrading brand of the shackles that he had worn. 'Yuh know," he continued to growl to his partners, the Hudson brothers, "Yuh know what this country needs more 'n anything else? It needs a good, hell-roarin' git-up and git-thar American town, and I'm goin' to start one, if you two jaspers will back me up."*

When the Hudson brothers agreed, the seed was sown that was to blossom into Eagle City. Their first recruit was Professor Howard, a white-bearded patriarch from a big eastern college who recommended the location for the proposed townsite. They were soon joined by Barney Gibbony, a saloon-man who had just made a big winning at the Dewey House and was looking for a good site to open a bar, Ed Martin and George Graves with his partner, One Thumb Jack, a pair of old-time gamblers with their own paraphernalia which included a faro outfit and roulette table. Jenny Moore sold out her small lunch counter business at the Forks to join the outfit, as did Becky White, a colored woman whose specialty was 'plain and fancy washing.' "Doc" Pernault was allured by the picture presented of the number of persons who usually needed medical attention in a wide-open American boom camp.

This motley crew shoved off in a large scow and four smaller river boats in semi-secrecy. To satisfy the curiosity of the nosey crowd, they hinted that they had had a belly full of the Klondike and were heading for Circle or Rampart or any other river port where all the country was not taken.

It was nearing noon the next day when they pulled into a bank directly opposite the little wooded island in mid-river that Professor Howard had described. Tents were hurriedly pitched, wood gathered and all preparations made for a permanent camp. A council was called after supper and Martin was elected chairman. While discussing a name for their town, an eagle soared overhead as though an omen, so the name was quickly settled. They decided to walk over their ground and when they returned to camp an hour later, the town and its streets were plotted and named.

During the next six weeks, the streets were cleared and lots were selected, all within a stone's throw of the civic center which was a large forty by sixty foot tent, bearing the name Barney Gibbony's American Saloon.

Darrell continued his story:

> *Three days later the river steamer, JOHN C. BARR, was flagged down and three of Eagle's leading citizens climbed aboard, their destination Dawson. The trio had in their possession the town's combined wealth, about four hundred ounces of gold dust, acceptable in Dawson at the exchange rate of sixteen dollars an ounce. Shortly after the boat landed in Dawson, a miner walked in Jack McDonald's and threw a poke of dust on the bar and called for drinks for the house. He made no secret of the fact that he had just come up river from the American side to pick up a few supplies. A request from the stranger that Jack McDonald take charge of his poke until he did some looking around caused a murmur of wonderment as he unslung two heavy moose hide pokes of dust on the bar and took McDonald's receipt for four hundred ounces.*
>
> *The dust was picked up later that afternoon, and after a quick transfer, the same performance was gone through by the other two Eagle-ites. One left a hundred and fifty ounces with the bartender at the Tivoli, while the other carelessly threw a two hundred and fifty ounce poke over the bar at Sam Bonnefils.*
>
> *The citizenry of Dawson began slipping towards their cabins and bunk houses and hastily threw the remnants of their outfits into boats, scows and onto hastily constructed rafts. Two days after the three citizens had slipped into Eagle, one jump ahead of the armada, the town's population leaped to near a thousand. Town lots went sky rocketing and claims on the creeks were at a premium. The Alaska Commercial Company dumped a load of logs off a big river scow to be used to erect a store. Eagle's fame was spreading.*

Darrell's story of the founding of Eagle City is confirmed by other early Eagle residents. M.D.K. Weimer, a newspaper reporter, wrote that Eagle City was settled by a group of American miners who were discontent with the Canadian taxes and laws and lack of available gold claims on the Klondike (Weimer, 1903). A letter dated 1897 was written by a prospector, which stated that he was heading down river to St. Michaels on his way home, but was spending the winter at Eagle City (Eagle Archives, Fogg).

EAGLE'S FIRST CIVIC CENTER
Courtesy: Art Knutson

Upon their arrival in Eagle City, the residents began clearing and
building cabins on their respective lots. It was estimated over
200 cabins were built during that first winter; most were crude one
room log cabins with pole and dirt roofs. A recorder was elected to
keep ownership records of the property. The recording fee was $5.
In 1898 the population had reached 700.

The main commercial center was a row of log cabins on "B" Street,
housing several saloons, gambling halls, restaurants and an Alaska
Commercial Company store.

B STREET, EAGLE CITY, 1898
Courtesy: National Archives

4

During this period, there were no government services available in the interior of Alaska, leaving the residents strictly on their own. There was no mechanism to incorporate a city or to provide law and order. During a public meeting on Feb. 2, 1898, the citizens formed a Chamber of Commerce and elected a Board of Trustees and Mayor. Mass meetings continued to be held to vote on irregular matters, major disputes or law infractions brought to their attention. The locals served as judge, jury and prosecutor. Major offenders found guilty were 'blue ticketed' and sent down river (Eagle City Records 1898). M.D.K. Weimer referred to these city meetings as miner's meetings, though they took care of much more business than similar ones held out on the creeks by a handful of miners.

By 1898 four large merchandising establishments had built stores and warehouses and each had their own fleet of sternwheelers. Eagle had survived its shaky beginnings and had become the commercial center for the surrounding gold fields due to its prime location on the river. A needed economic boost was received when the U.S. Army arrived in 1899 to build Fort Egbert adjacent to the City and the port of entry into Alaska was moved from Circle City to Eagle City.
In July 1900 Judge James Wickersham established the first Federal court in Alaska's interior, making Eagle the headquarters for the Third Judicial District. In January 1901 Eagle City became the first incorporated city in the interior of Alaska. An independent school district was also established during the incorporation election.

The five years following Judge Wickersham's arrival were the hey days of Eagle. It became the communications center when the first telegraph link was completed from Fort Egbert to Dawson in October 1900. By 1903 the telegraph line from Eagle to Valdez was completed, becoming part of the 1,497 mile WAMCATS (Washington-Alaska Military Cable and Telegraph System).

In 1903 a special subcommittee of the U. S. Senate Committee on Territories visited Alaska to gather information to assist them in wisely legislating matters about Alaska. Senators from Vermont, New Hampshire, Minnesota and Colorado arrived in Eagle on July 15th. They found a town with a population of 250, the home of the most northern U. S. Customs House and the most northern military post. They were especially impressed with the produce grown in the local gardens. They felt that Eagle was a town with a great future thus plans were made to build a railroad between Valdez and Eagle along the government mail trail and telegraph line. The local residents were eager for the Senators to support the railroad as well as a system of roads between Eagle and the Fortymile mining district (McLean, 1905:93).

Roald Amundsen, the famous Norwegian polar explorer, arrived in Eagle, Dec. 5, 1905, after mushing 1,000 miles by dog-team from Hershel Island where his sloop, the GJOA, was frozen in the Bering Sea. Amundsen remained in Eagle for two months, then mushed back to his ship and crew. (Amundsen 1928).

Dramatic changes in Eagle City began as early as 1904 when Judge Wickersham moved the headquarters for the Third Judicial District to Fairbanks following a major gold strike in that area. All of the larger trading companies with one exception had consolidated into one corporation to make their business profitable. With the adoption of the wireless in 1908, the telegraph line became obsolete and work at Fort Egbert slowed down. In 1911 Fort Egbert was abandoned except for a small Signal Corps detachment which remained to operate the wireless station until 1936.

The 1920 the U. S. Census of Eagle listed 98 residents, but only 50 in 1930 with the population swelling during the winter months when many of the miners moved into town. World War II and gasoline rationing put a halt to gold mining. Many of the miners went to Fairbanks to work in war time industries and the population dropped to nine residents one winter. With the completion of the Taylor Highway into Eagle in 1954, the population started growing again.

In 1970 Eagle was placed on the National Register of Historic Places and became a National Landmark in 1975. The five remaining buildings at Fort Egbert have been restored, as well as the original U. S. Courthouse and Custom's House. The Common Council of Eagle continues to hold their regular meetings in the 1901 City Hall building. Church services are held weekly in the historic church building. The State of Alaska operates a public school for grades K-12. Over 60 new buildings were built between 1971 and 1986. Most of them are log buildings so the general appearance of the community has not changed substantially. The grass airfield which had been constructed on Fort Egbert's parade grounds in the 1930's, has been replaced with a regulation gravel air field by the State of Alaska.

Though located on the banks of the Yukon River, Eagle City has been protected from flooding by its high bank. Erosion of this protective bank does occur from ice during a few of the breakups, from spring runoff from the city and scouring winds. During the May

1992 river-ice breakup, six to eight feet of river bank were lost in front of town. Front street was threatened as well as several historic buildings, residences and businesses. Thanks to two years of work by the City Council, the Soil Conservation Service constructed a two million dollar steel piling wall in front of town to protect the bank. With the completion of the work in Oct. 1994, the town is now protected and the appearance of Front Street greatly enhanced.

Of the 200 cabins built in Eagle during it's first year by the prospectors, most were crude one room log cabins with pole and dirt roofs. A few of the commercial buildings were constructed with lumber and had galvanized metal roofs.

During a mass meeting held on February 2, 1898, a plan for a town plat was adopted. A recorder was elected who drew up an application for a patent to the land included in the plat and sent it to Washington, D.C. Three to four hundred lots were staked and recorded, giving owners 30 days to brush the adjoining streets and one year to erect a building for which a fee of $5 was charged by the recorder. A receipt was given for payment. The first recorder retired with his earnings and a second recorder was elected.

Everything went smoothly until a murmur arose over paying anyone to settle on U. S. domain as the sellers could show no more authority for land ownership than merely measuring off 50'x 150' lots. Others, wanting to divide the spoils, jumped the lower end of the town site, cleared the streets and made more extensive preparations with better rules and regulations.

On May 26, 1898, during another mass meeting, the residents adopted a new and very different plan for the town plat for the portion of ground north of Adams Street. The elected recorder used a small pocket compass and a cheap cloth tape line for measuring the streets and lots locations for individuals who were willing to pay the recording fee (Eagle City Records, 1898).

The second recorder left with a heavy gold sack, with plans to get his plat recognized as a government townsite, be appointed its Commissioner and reap further rewards. Unfortunately the application was disallowed as not being in accordance with the law. Finally they were told by the Secretary of the Interior that their application could be granted if an efficient civil government was provided, but he knew of no laws under which towns in Alaska could be incorporated. The application was redated and resubmitted, only to be ignored again (Eagle City Records, 1898).

During 1898, many city lots changed hands, selling as low as $10 to $25 and as high as $2500 for a prime river front business site. The average price was $50 to $100 with business establishments on "B" Street bringing a standard $500.

During the summer of 1899 U. S. Deputy surveyor, E. J. Chamberlain arrived in Eagle and prepared an official town plat. He reported that the measurements and alignments previously made were through timber and dense underbrush, consequently the stakes were far from straight lines. From those which were on nearly level ground, he was able to make the necessary adjustments without disturbing any

EAGLE CITY PLANNERS, 1900. l-r FORD, HOBBS,
x, QUARRY, MANCHESTER, BARTLETT, x, COLEMAN
Courtesy: Harriett Ford Henderson

large buildings or improvements (Eagle City Records, 1899).

During the summer of 1901, the exterior boundaries of the townsite of Eagle were surveyed by Corporal Theo. Lentz at Fort Egbert. The lines surveyed by him were cleared of brush and trees from four to six feet wide. The town plat had included much of the flat ground which the army had intended to use. There were 38 cabin sites on the land acquired by the Army for their Fort, which caused many protests from the residents. The army gave the owners permission to move the cabins to another location or offered to buy each for twenty-five dollars.

One of the army's responsibilities in establishing Fort Egbert in 1899 was to provide law and order and the military reservation for the proposed fort included the Eagle townsite, since the town was without a legal civil government. The nearest civil officer, a custom's agent, was 160 miles away at Circle City. This gave the military authorities of the post full jurisdiction over the Eagle area. Now it was necessary for residents seeking property within the reservation to obtain permission from the Fort Commander. In March 1900, the reservation was extended to include all lands to the Canadian border, approximately 25,600 acres.

As a result of the Alaska Civil Code which was passed by the U. S. Congress in June 1900, a civil government was established by Judge Wickersham. Under this new law, the City of Eagle petitioned for an incorporation election November 10, 1900 and the election was held January 1901. With a legal civil government now in place, the military reservation was modified to exclude the Eagle City Townsite. As an incorporated town, Eagle would become responsible for its own policing, sanitation and other municipal activities which would mean taxation to pay for the services. The commercial companies, figuring that the taxes would fall mostly on them, opposed the incorporation and separation from the military reservation. The commanding officer at Fort Egbert, Colonel Ray, wrote in his diary, "It is amusing to see how the zeal for freedom from military oppression is smothered by the discovery that the alternative is taxation."

Though many of the first prospectors had drifted off in search of richer gold fields, Eagle was a growing town. By June 1902, twenty buildings had been completed at Fort Egbert and others were under construction. There was a U.S. Courthouse and a U.S. Jail, both frame buildings. Two large commercial companies had frame stores and sheet iron warehouses. There were nine other frame buildings, about 200 log houses, two churches, five saloons, one hotel and two restaurants. The population was estimated to be 300. The older houses, with dirt-covered roofs for warmth and moss calked cracks between the logs, wore flower gardens on their tops like gay spring bonnets, very picturesque and jaunty.

U. G. Myers was appointed Trustee for Townsite entry of lands in Eagle by the Secretary of the Interior on September 15, 1903. Application for the townsite of Eagle was once again made. A deposit of $750 was required to pay for surveying the boundaries of the townsite. To raise the money, each acre of land was assessed $1.25 on May 1907. A call for bids to subdivide the townsite was issued and three bids were received. F.E.G. Berry's bid for $975, being the lowest, was accepted and a contract was entered into on June 18, 1908 for subdividing 320 acres. The survey was completed in July 1908, checked by the trustee on August 3rd and 4th and posted for 30 days. Allotments were made September 10th and 11th, 1908.

On March 2, 1909, the trustee received a telegram stating, "All land in entry patented January 18, 1909. Proceed as if patent received." Mr. Myers began to distribute deeds dated April 1, 1909 and the Eagle residents received their first official deed to their land. The City of Eagle later received a Townsite Patent which was signed by President Theodore Roosevelt January 18, 1909 with a seal and large red ribbon.

ULYSSES G. MYERS
1867-1918

The one person most actively involved with Eagle property in the early days was U. G. Myers. He wore many hats while living in Eagle where he had been sent in 1899 by the U. S. Weather Bureau. He signed the city petition for incorporation in 1900 and was elected the first mayor by the city council after incorporation. He remained on the city council until 1918, serving as mayor, clerk, municipal magistrate, coroner, election clerk and election judge. He worked as a lawyer, broker and notary public and served as the U. S. Commissioner and Recorder until his death in 1918.

September 15, 1903, Myers was appointed Trustee for the Townsite entry of lands in Eagle under commission from the Secretary of Interior and served in that capacity until the individual deeds were distributed to the property owners in 1909. Myers and his wife, Nellie, built one of the nicest log homes in Eagle known as 'The Birches', where they enjoyed entertaining many visitors. Myers was an active member in the Arctic Brotherhood and Improved Order of Red Men lodges.

During the summer of 1918 Mrs. Myers returned home to Poughkeepsie, New York for a visit. U. G. decided to join her for the winter and took the last boat up river in 1918. Boarding at Skagway, he was among those on the ill fated S. S. Sophia that went down in Lynn Canal October 25, 1918, losing all on board. At the time of his death he was 51 years of age. His friend, Bert Bryant wrote, "U. G. was one of the best men I ever met, taken from all angles. His loss was irreparable."

More was learned about the Myers family from the deposition which Mrs. Myers made, while filing a claim with the Canadian Pacific Railway Company, owners of the Steamship 'Princess Sophia' (National Archives).

Myers was born October 1867 in Pennsylvania and was a graduate of William and Mary College. After graduation, he trained at Fort Meyer, Washington, D. C. for the United States Weather Bureau (then under the War Department). He served in the U. S. Weather Bureau for a number of years and was sent to Eagle, Alaska in 1899. While in Eagle he studied law, passed the bar examination and began practicing law in 1906. He continued his law practice at Eagle, in particular serving as counsel for several mining companies. He severed his connection with the U. S. Weather Bureau when he was appointed U. S. Commissioner and Recorder at Eagle in 1906.

Myers was at his office at the Courthouse in Eagle every working day. There was no Deputy Commissioner so he did all of the work of that office, which required many hearings. He was also the official recorder, and having no clerk, he personally had to attend to recording all the mining claims. When not actually engaged in his duties as Commissioner and Recorder, he devoted his time to his private practice. In the summer when boats from Dominion, Y. T., Canada were in port at Eagle, he worked as a custom house broker. He spent many evenings at his work either at home or at his office. Myers never drank and his only recreation was a short hunting trip. He was in perfect health up to the time of his death.

"THE BIRCHES", HOME OF U. G. MYERS.
Courtesy: Sheldon Museum, Haines

While observer for the Weather Bureau, Myers received about $3,500 per year. As U. S. Commissioner and Recorder, he was entitled to fees up to $3,000 per year. He averaged about $2,500 each summer as customs house broker and about the same amount from his private law practice.

Myers laid aside no salary or accumulations. He spent half of his earnings in living and other expenses and the remainder upon the various mining enterprises. Myers outfitted many prospectors, sending them out to prospect and do the assessment work on located claims, paying all expenses in return for a shared interest in the claim. Mrs. Myers knew of over 50 such claims, every one of them costing him from $100 to $500 and several in excess of $500.

Mrs. Myers was born April 1872 in New York and married Myers in 1899. She had lived in Eagle for 14 continuous years and took over the U. S. Weather Bureau position after her husband resigned. For this work she received $1,200 per year. She continued this position until 1911 when the Fort was closed.

The Myers had no children and no parents survived U. G. His widow Nellie was his only heir. U. G.'s body was recovered and buried at Saney Hill, Pennsylvania.

Following Myers death, his wife returned to Eagle only once, to settle their business, selling as much of their Eagle property as possible. In 1919, she took over Harry Ross's mining interests on Alder Creek, though she was living in New York at the time. She later married Mr. Parsons.

CHAPTER 2

JUDICIAL SYSTEM

After the United States purchased Alaska from Russia in 1867, only
a skeleton government was set up in Sitka; nothing was provided
for the interior area. As the first groups of miners arrived and
problems arose, they banded together and held miner's meetings
where disputes were settled, murderers hung and lesser culprits
sent out of the area on the first boat.

This worked well until the population increased so much that such
meetings became so numerous and large that it was questioned if
justice was being accomplished. Too often the popular man came out
victorious. Having a miner's meeting every few days, gave the town
a name for being unlawful and unruly and one of the worst camps on
the river.

Some of the citizens suggested that a Judicial District be established by forming a court and electing the necessary officers at a
general election. The town already had a Mayor, Councilmen and a
Police Judge selected by the Chamber of Commerce, but some matters
came up which could not be disposed of by this body. This formed
two factions in the community, one in favor of miner's rule, the
other in favor of law and order. An active canvas was made, and
each had their respective tickets. In the spring election, a common
man was elected judge instead of his opponent, a lawyer.

With all of the publicity which Alaska was receiving due to the
gold rush, the United States Legislature finally extended the
United States governing bodies to the Northern District. An Alaska
Civil Code was passed in June 1900 which divided Alaska into three
judicial districts. Eagle was selected as the headquarters for the
third judicial district and James Wickersham was appointed the
Judge. He arrived in Eagle in July 1900 with his family and members
of the Court. With a civil government in place, the military
reservation was modified to exclude the Eagle City Townsite.

Wickersham remained in Eagle until there was a stampede to new gold
fields in the Tanana Valley and the city population dwindled. In
the spring of 1904, he moved the court headquarters to Fairbanks.
After that date, the judicial business was carried on in Eagle by
a Deputy United States Marshal and United States Commissioner.

The Commissioners held circuit courts with the full authority of a
Probate Judge. They were appointed by the District Judge and
received no salary, but could keep the fees up to $3,000 a year for
compensation. As a Justice of the Peace, they could try civil cases
where the amount involved was less than $1,000 and could try
criminal cases and sentence up to a year's imprisonment. More
serious cases had to be tried by the District Judge in Fairbanks.
The Commissioners acted as coroners, notaries and recorders of
their precinct.

The Deputy United States Marshals were kept busy performing the duties of constables, investigating murders, rapes, thefts, smuggling, claim jumpers, lost persons, etc. and bringing in the criminals.

JAMES WICKERSHAM

President McKinley selected James Wickersham as the Judge for the Third District with his headquarters in Eagle City. At the time of his appointment, he was a lawyer and city attorney in Tacoma, Washinton.

Accompanying Wickersham north were his wife, Debbie and their seven year old son, Howard. Darrell, their oldest son, was attending the Annapolis Naval Academy. Arthur, the middle son, had passed away some years earlier.

The party traveled by steamship to Skagway, over the mountain pass on the nearly completed White Pass and Yukon Railroad and then by sternwheeler from Lake Bennett to Eagle City where they arrived July 15, 1900. They were greeted by the entire Eagle population, 385 white and native residents, including the Mayor, Mr. Quarry, who helped them get settled.

There was much court work to be done. Their area of jurisdiction covered 300,000 square miles and contained 1,500 white residents plus the natives. There was not a courthouse, regular jail, school nor other public building in the area and not a mile of public wagon road or trail for transportation. The day after their arrival in town, the Judge and Clerk started levying business fees. The annual fee for a saloon license was $1,000 and mercantile licenses were a fixed percentage of their annual sales. At that time there were five saloons and three large stores (Wickersham 1938:41).

The Judge authorized two town lots to be reserved for a courthouse and jail. The construction of a courthouse, not to exceed $5,000, was to be paid for by the local license fees. Men started cutting logs and permission was received to use the military sawmill which was standing idle. On February 2, 1901, the contract was let to build the courthouse and jail which were completed May 10, 1901. Young Howard Wickersham raised the flag on the most northern American Courthouse.

While work was proceeding on the courthouse, Wickersham built a log cabin for his family across the street. He enjoyed the outdoor activities, and found time to hunt for moose and caribou as well as prospect for gold. He even filed on some mining claims.

Before the first winter set in, Wickersham, accompanied by Debbie and Howard, held court in Rampart and Circle. By November, Mrs. Wickersham held her first afternoon tea for the ladies of the town and settled into the social life. Later in the month, Wickersham and his wife attended a ball at Fort Egbert, held in the barracks drill hall. It was the big social event of the season and Wickersham dressed in formal attire including his swallow-tail coat.

16

After the holidays, he set out on his first mid-winter circuit with
a dog team and snowshoes, a 1,140 miles round trip to Circle and
Rampart in minus 50 and 60 degree weather. The trip took 45 days
of which twelve were spent out-of-doors in the crisp Arctic cold.
He soon found that winter was a good time for court travel, but not
without some discomforture. In February he wrote, "42 degrees
below....I hurt my ankle by a fall the first day out....is paining
me badly and is very swollen. Raised a bad blister on my other foot
trying to shield the bad ankle; opened the blister and filled the
hole with coal oil from one of the lanterns which seems to effect

JUDGE JAMES WICKERSHAM'S HOME IN EAGLE 1900
l-r MRS. WICKERSHAM, THE JUDGE, MRS. HEILIG
Courtesy: Eagle historical Society

a rapid cure" (Wickersham 1938:62). Even the spring travel caused
him some problems with all the bright sunshine. "March 22.......
today I am suffering greatly with snow blindness. My eyes feel as
if they are filled with sand and I keep them covered with a bandage

17

and hold onto the handle bars of the sled for guidance" (Wickersham 1938:76).

During the winter months which Wickersham spent in Eagle, he used much of his time on a variety of intellectual pursuits. A study club was organized during which the members read papers they had prepared. In December Wickersham presented a paper on the history of Alaska. At one of the study club meetings, a committee was appointed to consider the establishment of a public library in Eagle and Wickersham assisted with the organization. He also worked with the Indians in the village, in an effort to put their language in written form.

When Wickersham accepted his Alaskan assignment from President McKinley, he had paid his own and his family's traveling expenses from Tacoma, built his own cabin, supported his family and paid official expenses out of his own pocket. His annual salary was $5,000 but their first paychecks didn't arrive until February 1901, eight months after their departure from Seattle. The checks only covered five months of their employment and continued to be three to four months in arrears. Fortunately, the Alaska Commercial Company extended credit to the financially embarrassed officials.

Dispensing justice where none had existed previously, demanded an innovative imagination. Assisting the Judge in Eagle were a court clerk, official stenographer, United States attorney, Assistant United States Attorney, United States District Attorney and license collector, United States Marshal, Deputy United States Marshal and United States Commissioner. There were also Deputy Marshals and Commissioners at the larger mining camps within the judicial district.

There was no shortage of attorneys to represent the citizens. In 1901 there were eight members of the bar in Eagle, eleven in 1903 and fourteen in 1905. Wickersham wrote that the behavior of the jurors was a problem when he first took over the Alaska Bench. "They were unalterably lenient in their verdicts and vulnerable to bribery and blackmail, refusing to return an indictment. The problem was partially due to the system by which jurors were impanelled. The selection of the jurors was made by the U.S. Marshal and his choice was often influenced by his judgment as to the guilt of the accused. The attorneys did not hesitate to confer with the Marshal as well as with the jurors, on behalf of their clients."

During the summer of 1903, Wickersham traveled to the Aleutian Islands by boat where he held court while Debbie and Howard returned to Tacoma. That winter, Wickersham was sent to Nome to hold court, to relieve the corrupt judge involved in the gold scandal. While in Nome, Wickersham received word that his young son Howard, had died from pleurisy, typhoid fever and tuberculosis. The Judge was heart broken. Debbie also suffered from

tuberculosis and went to Annapolis to visit their remaining son
Darrell. Due to her poor health, Debbie remained in Tacoma and her
visits to Alaska became rare.

Upon his return to Eagle, Wickersham found the population in the
area had diminished due to the stampede to new gold strikes in the
Tanana Valley. He telegraphed the Attorney-General and recommended
that the headquarters of the court be moved from Eagle to the new
mining district of Fairbanks. This was accomplished in the spring
of 1904.

After years of hardwork on the bench and with his wife's health
deteriorating, Wickersham submitted his resignation as a federal
judge to become effective March 1, 1908. He was admitted to the
Alaska bar and he opened a law office in Fairbanks. That same year
he was elected Delegate to Congress thus continuing his life of
public service.

Bob Steel came into the country in 1897 before his 18th birthday, arriving in Valdez with his brother.   Traveling winters and prospecting summers, it took them two years to get to the Fortymile River gold fields.   His brother moved on to Fairbanks, but Bob remained for two more years and then moved to Eagle where he worked for the United States Army as a packer, helping to string the telegraph wire from Eagle to Valdez.   He was in charge of the supply outfit and knowing the morse code, he would cut in at night and keep the headquarters informed on their progress and conditions.

In 1908, Beatrice Gustin, a young girl, came to Eagle to visit her sister, Mrs. Clyde Thompson, who was her only living relative. An attractive single girl in town created a real stir where there were ten men for every woman. Working in the Thompson roadhouse didn't interfere with Bea's busy social life, which included dances, berry picking parties, church, buggy or sleigh rides, long walks, climbing the bluff, playing on the girl's basketball team in the military gymnasium and evenings of cards, music and conversation. Among her many admirers who were competing for her attention, was Bob Steel. After one winter, Bea tired of Alaska and returned to Seattle. Bob followed her and they were married in Seattle on August 7, 1909. Though they had planned to make their home in Seattle, those plans went awry and they returned to Eagle.

Bob was trying his hand at mining so the couple moved to the Fortymile River where he worked on the dredge for two seasons. Their first child was born in Dawson. Bob now had a family to support and found the best source of a steady income was with the government. He started as a game warden for the Eagle, Fortymile and Circle Districts. Among the game laws was the prohibition of hunting ducks in the spring. In 1916, if you didn't hunt ducks in the spring, you could be pretty hungry, especially the Indians for whom the game laws also applied. There was a law that a prospector out in the hills was allowed to shoot game when he needed meat, to prevent starvation. He didn't need to be told he could; he would have done it anyway.

Bob's family in California kept writing of all the work that was available there. So Bob and Bea moved to California where their third daughter was born in 1917. Bea had hoped they would remain outside, but Bob decided he preferred Alaska to California and they returned to Eagle City once again. In 1918 Bob bought into some mining property on the Seventymile River, though he continued working as the game warden.

After returning, Bob found better paying government jobs to support his family, such as the United States Deputy Marshal. While serving in that capacity, Bob had to pick up a man who was declared

BEA GUSTIN & ROBERT STEEL COURTING 1908
Courtesy: Lucilla Cameron

insane. He had attacked one man and just about finished Bob off before he was subdued and handcuffed. The patient was shipped out to Morningside, a mental institution in Oregon.

Next Bob was appointed Postmaster and served in that position from 1920-1941. During that time he was also appointed United States Commissioner and held court in the Wickersham Courthouse. Bea served as the Postmaster whenever Bob was working as the Marshal or Commissioner.

Bea was an excellent cook and a hard working mother, raising eight children. Upon demand, she started a boarding house after Bobby Beggs bought the only hotel (Riverside) in town in 1922, as only Percy DeWolfe would stay with him. In order to accommodate the boarders, the Steels purchased the big two story Heath Hotel and turned it into a roadhouse. Bob put siding over the exterior logs and insulated the building with sawdust. He added a kitchen and another room on the back. When the children were older, he built a bunk house in back for them. Bea had six to ten regular boarders, plus the travelers.

Bob provided cold storage by digging a tunnel into the ground until he hit ice (permafrost) and then by digging out a large room. In the winter, he would fill it with blocks of river ice which remained frozen throughout the summer. They could also keep frozen meat frozen in the cold room, but it wouldn't freeze fresh meat. They had a large garden and hothouse and could store their winter vegetables in the cold room. In addition they planted an entire city block in potatoes. In the road-house, they served garden vegetables and wild meat. It was a real treat to have a turkey for the holidays.

Near the road-house, the Steels had a dog barn, as Bob used dog teams for winter travel. He also kept horses for which he raised oat hay and cut wild hay which was mixed for their feed. He burned off the hay fields each spring and was able to cut three tons of wild hay for each horse.

The Steel Road-house became the town's community center. It contained the postoffice which received three mail deliveries a month. Teachers roomed there and many of the bachelors in town took their meals there on a regular basis. Bridge games were the order of the evening after dinner. All of the Signal Corps men were at the road house playing bridge the evening the telegraph station on the hill burned to the ground. There was a player piano which Mr. Steel enjoyed playing. Miners walked in from the creeks and stayed a few days while getting supplies or while waiting for transportation else-where.

Bob was elected to the City Council from 1917-1928, and served as assessor and school tax collector. Bea was active on the school board, chairing the board in 1937. Bob was active in the Improved Order of Redmen organization which held weekly socials in their hall and sponsored many community programs.

Years rolled by swiftly and the eight children were growing up. The school in Eagle only went through the 8th grade, so the older children had to leave home to attend high school. The first girl went to Seattle, the second attended a parochial boarding school in Dawson for $30 a month, while the 3rd lived with a family in Fairbanks and worked for her room and board. In 1937 when the two youngest boys were ready for high school and the oldest daughter was attending the University of Alaska, Fairbanks, Bea decided to move into Fairbanks. They bought a large house and at first rented out rooms. Later Bob added third and fourth floors with lumber from the Fort Egbert buildings, making it into the Steel Hotel which Bea operated.

Bob remained in Eagle to run their road-house, with the help of his older daughters. While he was in Fairbanks working on the hotel, one daughter had to be acting Postmaster, but she was not supposed to assume the commissioner's work. She didn't know that when Gus Douglas' bride arrived in Eagle. When Bob returned home he was surprised to learn that his daughter had sold them a marriage license and they had been married. Bob just laughed. He remained in Eagle until he was able to sell the road-house to his nephew, Guilbert Thompson and then he joined Bea in Fairbanks where they operated the Steel Hotel together until the 1950's.

Bea finally got her way and the Steels moved to Washington. She chose not to travel with Bob, who returned to Fairbanks every summer and wintered in warmer climes, California or Mexico.
Bob died at the age of 84 and was buried in the Steel family plot in Berkeley, California. Bea lived to be 83 years old when she died of cancer in 1972 while visiting her children in Alaska. She was buried in Anchorage.

CHAPTER 3

CUSTOMS SERVICE

The United States Customs Service under the Department of Internal Revenue, was the first official government agency in the Upper Yukon. In 1897 Circle city was the port of Entry. After Eagle City was established, it was possible to have a site closer to the international border, so the office was moved to Eagle.

During the summer months, the seven Customs collectors worked around the clock. At Eagle, every boat from Dawson and the Klondike had to stop to enter the ship and settle dues for the foreign goods brought in their hold. As many as five sternwheelers with their square nosed barges laden with goods, were tied up at Eagle at one time. The Captains were impatient as the season was short; they would pace up and down the bank swearing at the delay caused by the customs inspections.

When the river froze and the traffic was lighter, some of the collectors were sent south to work during the winter. After 1944 the river traffic had so decreased, the Postmasters served as the Customs Agents.

The Customs Agents had many duties besides checking on incoming merchandise. They were often sent to investigate reports of smuggled goods, mainly cigars, tobacco and woolens. They often received messages to be on the lookout for specific individuals who were wanted for various reasons, i.e. theft, murder., rape, etc. Another duty was to check on passports for incoming persons.

Outbreaks of epidemics such as diphtheria and smallpox were closely monitored. If these occurred in Dawson, all incoming passengers from that area were held in quarantine until after the incubation period passed, and they would then receive a health certificate for entrance into Alaska. Quarantine camps were established in Eagle and supervised by a health officer.

Animals also had to be checked when they entered Alaska. Tuberculin tests were given and mallein was administered to test for glanders. The horses were held in quarantine until the results were determined.

After Fort Egbert was abandoned in 1911, many of the buildings became available for other uses. One of the Non-commissioned Officers quarters was transferred to the United States Treasury Department in 1915 for use as a customs office. The building was moved to the city waterfront where the boats tied up. It provided space for the customs offices as well as quarters for single agents and room for social gatherings. The old Customs House remained empty after 1944, so it was transferred to the City of Eagle in 1968 for use as a museum.

CLARENCE L. ANDREWS
1862-1948

C. L. Andrews played a key role in Eagle's history where he worked as the Chief Customs Service Collector from 1904 to 1909. He was also an author and photographer and left an outstanding record of Eagle during that period. He was always making notes in his diary which he used later in his writings. He published The Story of Alaska, The Story of Sitka, Wrangell and the Gold of the Cassiar, and Nuggets of Verse Panned from the Gravels of the Past plus many magazine articles.

Andrews was born in 1862 and lived on a farm in Ohio until the age of two, when his family moved to Oregon. They had traveled by water and his father died on the way and was buried at sea. Andrews was raised in the Willamette Valley, attended the United Brethren College and graduated in business in 1882. He spent the next 17 years between Seattle and parts of Oregon working as county clerk, auditor and farmer. He married Anne M. Anderson in 1885; his wife died in childbirth August 6, 1886. That same year he married Ida and raised a family. During a visit his wife and three children drowned in a flood in Oregon in 1903.

Andrews first came to Alaska in 1892. He returned in 1897 with the Luigi Expedition as a bearer and camp hand to climb Mt. St. Elias which is located on the Alaska-Canada border. Joining the Customs Service, he spent one year in Sitka, five years in Skagway during the gold rush and was sent to Eagle in 1904. He retired from the service in 1909 and worked as a freelance writer in Sitka. From 1923 to 1929 he worked in Alaska's Arctic for the Bureau of Indian Affairs School and Reindeer Service.

Andrews left for Eagle on March 4, 1904 and arrived on the 20th where he went to work immediately as the custom's service was busy as blazes. The river was beautiful when they had time to look at it. He took his meals at the hotel which Miss Thompson was operating in her jovial manner. Great strong wolf-like dogs stood in the streets and eyed him as he passed. Their half wild ways and yellow eyes made one doubtful of their intentions. The soldiers went up and down the streets in groups of two and three.

Andrews took many photographs and developed his plates at the home of Frank Smith, manager of the Northern Commercial Company. Andrews made short observations of the town in his diary, using them in his later publications (UAF Archives: Andrews). "People's scow and Haraden's scow were in during the morning. Large rafts of logs were floated down river to the sawmill. Many missed the landing and rafts broke up losing the logs. Bought a birch bark basket for fifty cents. Grey wolf and wolverine skins sell for only $30. In August enjoyed fresh vegetables from Woodruff's and Dr. Clayton's gardens. Mrs. Lundquist arrived with her cow on a scow. Got a drink of fresh cow milk for only fifty cents a quart. Salmon were running; Indians sell them for thirty cents each. Attended Bevington's wedding reception. Had to make an official investigation trip. While in Fairbanks met Judges Harlan and Wickersham, Hess, Heilig and daughter and Dr. Hall."

Andrews' activities continued to be well recorded. "First of April 1905 attended Arctic Brotherhood concert in the evening. Next day five of the men and I went down river with dog sled to the third island. Catching white fish through the ice by the bluff. Hospital Sgt. David returned from Fort Yukon with frozen feet and had to have some toes amputated. He went down to see about Indians with diphtheria, lost his way in the flats and got frozen. April 30th the wild crocus in bloom."

The manger of the Northern Commercial store, Frank and Mrs. Smith had a teenage daughter, Lidlie, whose name began appearing frequently in Andrews' diary. Andrews confided in his diary, "Lidlie dearer to me every day." Later in the month after an evening of chess, Andrews wrote, "The world is a pretty good place and Eagle has its pleasures as well as Coney Island. Although some might think it dull, I'm glad I'm here this winter."

"On Dec. 6th, Captain Amundsen and Captain Mogg called on me. On Dec. 9th Captain Mogg went to Dawson; Jules Marion and Captain Amundsen went later. Dec. 19th, Arctic Brotherhood meeting; Captain Amundsen made honorary member."

"January 6th, 1906 at mess house in afternoon. (Northern Commercial Co. operated a mess house where the Smith family lived with a Chinese cook. Amundsen roomed with them [Amundsen 1928]). On Jan 9th, went calling with Captain Amundsen in the afternoon. February 2, 1906, Captain Amundsen getting ready to go. At mess hall in evening. Feb. 3rd Captain Amundsen left for his boat at 8:30 a.m. Feb. 22nd went sledding on toboggan with Lidlie and Murray and they got hurt. How I wish I could help some way."

When Andrews moved to Seattle in 1909, the United States Department of Interior hired him to travel in Alaska to gather material for the Alaska-Yukon-Pacific Exposition in Seattle. For the next fourteen years he continued to gather material in Alaska for his writing and to expand his collection of photographs. In 1923 he settled at Kivalina as a teacher with the U. S. Bureau of Education and Reindeer Service. In 1926, three years before his retirement, he was appointed reindeer superintendent at Nome.

Though Andrews had left Eagle in 1909, he maintained his relationship with Lidlie and they were married March 10, 1914. He took her to New York and Connie Island on their honeymoon. It is not known how the marriage ended, but Andrews married Eva Alvey in 1918. Andrews spent his later years in Sitka and Oregon. He died in 1948 at his sisters in Oregon.

JOHN J. 'JACK' HILLARD
1873-1961

From the mouth of the Yukon, up the Tanana River and over the
Alaska Railroad to Fairbanks, Jack Hillard was affectionately known
as 'Old Man River.' He had spent nearly forty-four years as the
American Customs officer at Eagle, so the name was fitting.

Hillard first came to Alaska in 1898 as a member of the crew of a
fishing schooner out of San Francisco. Upon returning to the Bay
area in the fall, he enrolled at the University of California. Upon
completion of his courses, he passed his Civil Service exams for
the Customs Service.

From 1900 to 1911 when Fort Egbert was occupied, Eagle was a busy
port of call with as many as five sternwheelers at the docks at any
one time and as many Customs officials working around the clock.
After the closure of Fort Egbert, traffic down the Yukon began to
dwindle, so the number of Customs Officers was dropped to one.

Hillard would arrive at Eagle on the first boat in the spring and
depart on the last boat each fall before the river froze. During
the winters he was stationed in San Francisco at the Customs House
until his wife, Betty, died. After that, he spent his winters
relieving other Customs Officers along the Southeastern Alaska
coast who took their vacations during the winter months. This also
included Fairbanks thus he became well known in Southeastern Alaska
as well as in the interior of Alaska.

During the fall of 1918, Jack was in Skagway on assignment at the
time of the sinking of the S. S. Princess Sophia - the Canadian
vessel that went aground on Vanderbilt Reef between Haines and
Juneau. It was a terrible disaster with the loss of all the crew
and passengers aboard. As the bodies were found, they were taken
to Juneau to be cleaned, identified and embalmed. The S. S.
Princess Alice was sent from Juneau to Skagway to pick up men and
equipment to take them to Juneau to assist in handling the corpses.
Hillard and another Customs Agent were also picked up to assist in
identifying the bodies. This was one of the most unpleasant tasks
of Hillard's entire career with the Custom's Service. Many of the
corpses he identified were his friends (Coates 1991:112).

The Hillards had no children until they adopted Cora Thompson's
baby, Bill. In 1925, when Bill was six years old, the Hillards
took out formal papers adopting young Jack Willis Thompson. Bill
considered himself one of the luckiest people who ever got their
start in Eagle. Each winter he went to California with his parents
and returned to Eagle each summer. His Mother and he had a horse,
Black Joe, which he rode every summer. Thanks to Jack Hillard his
childhood seemed an ideal one.

It was not uncommon during prohibition for bottles of liquor to be confiscated from the passengers on the boats crossing the border into Alaska. Jack Hillard, being an obliging person, had made arrangements with the White Pass and Yukon Route, to allow ship departures from Dawson at a more convenient hour. This put the boats arrival in Eagle during the early hours of the morning and the passengers sleep was not disturbed. Hillard boarded the ships in Dawson, thus giving him the opportunity to size up the passengers before crossing the boundary line in Alaska. Having had years of experience he seldom missed in figuring who would be the passenger or passengers who were trying to sneak more than the incidental bottle across the border. When he did find contraband, it would be lifted and put into his safe in the office.

Jack made many friends during his years in Alaska. He was very fond of the Thompson family and the children. One year when he returned to Eagle, he brought them a pony. He always kept a horse which he generously allowed friends to ride. He took a special interest in the second set of Thompson children by seeing that the two eldest were sent to mission schools in later years.

Jack had many famous visitors in Eagle. He was host to Roald Amundsen, the first to take a boat through the Northwest Passage and the locator of the South Pole. Amundsen came to Eagle to telegraph home and to get provisions to take back to his crew frozen in the ice. It was at this time that Jack loaned his pride and joy, Happy, to Amundsen for his lead dog on his way back to his ship, the Gjoa. Happy was later returned to Hillard in San Francisco.

Hillard retired in 1944 to a small home in San Leandro, California. He kept in contact with his Alaskan friends and many of them visited him. He had been the first man in Eagle to own an automobile. First it was a 1916 touring car and then a 1927 Oakland. You can imagine Hillard's surprise when Jess and Cathryne Knight drove up to his front door at Oakland in 1945 with his old 1927 Oakland which they had driven from the interior of Alaska. First they had to raft the car down the Yukon River from Eagle to Circle to connect with the highway

Jack died in 1961 at the age of 88. Horace Biederman and Susie Paul scattered his ashes on the frozen Yukon opposite the Customs House while saying the Lord's Prayer.

CHAPTER 4

COMMERCIAL ESTABLISHMENTS

As the commercial companies entered the Upper Yukon, they began to establish trading posts. One trader was Francois Mercier, who as an employee of the Western Fur and Trading Company in 1880, established a trading post near present day Eagle (Mercier 1986:3). After the Klondike gold discovery in 1896, life changed rapidly on the Upper Yukon. Prospectors and miners infiltrated the entire countryside, establishing many gold rush towns. Soon the traders were catering to the prospectors rather than the Indians.

Eagle attracted many business operators who built log stores on B Street between Front and 1st Streets. The Alaska Commercial Company was among the first to open a store in a log building and was soon joined by many saloons, boarding houses and restaurants. ACC's business soon outgrew the log cabin and they moved across the street and built a large 30'x 90" one story frame building with a corrugated iron warehouse the same size attached to the river side of the building.

ALASKA COMMERCIAL CO. STORE & POSTOFFICE
WHICH LATER BECAME THE NCCO.
Courtesy: Eagle Historical Society

Eagle was booming. ACC shipped out $750,000 in gold at the end of the 1900 mining season. Having become the commercial center for the adjoining gold fields, ACC was soon joined by the North American Transportation and Trading Company, the Alaska Exploration Company and the Seattle-Yukon Transportation Company plus several locally own and operated stores. All of the major commercial companies operated their own sternwheelers on the Yukon River.

By 1901, no transportation company in the North broke even. The Alaska Commercial Company realized that without any profit, all of the major businesses would be out of business, leaving Alaska without river transportation or even supplies. Duplicate overheads, identical routes and services were losing money for all the river shipping lines. Negotiations began that same year, and the Alaska Commercial Company, Alaska Exploration Company and the Empire Transportation Company combined under the name of Northern Commercial Company, which bought out the Seattle-Yukon Transportation Co. A second corporation was organized, the Northern Navigation Co., exclusively for transportation and shipping. Steamboats of the North America Transportation & Trading Co. operated with this combination for awhile and then withdrew and operated separately, until the Northern Commercial Co. bought them out in 1912.

Following this merger, Eagle was served by the one large corporation plus several small local stores. John Paulson had opened a general store and lodging house in 1898. He was joined by Charlie Ott in 1903 and the name was changed to Paulson and Ott. Paulson sold his share of the store to John Scheele, a tinsmith, in 1908 and the store became Ott and Scheele. They had a good business, so they enlarged the log warehouse and store building where Charlie Ott lived. Another local business was operated by Peoples and Woodruff.

Besides the general merchandise companies, there were two hotels, the Heath Hotel and Riverside Hotel.

BLAKE D. MILLS

Blake D. Mills lived in Eagle from 1899-1903. He was in charge of
the Seattle-Yukon Transportation Company store and was also elected
mayor before Eagle was incorporated as a City. The following are
excerpts from his autobiographical account written in 1930 about
his life in Eagle.

"While in Dawson in 1898, I met Judge W. D. Wood of the Seattle-
Yukon Transportation Co. and he hired me to go to work for them.
The next spring, I sailed up the Yukon on the Seattle #3, loaded to
the guard rails with supplies for the three stores. The amount of
goods for Eagle was very limited. They were placed on the river
bank, a tarpaulin put over them and the Seattle #3 moved on
upstream.

"Judge Wood had purchased several lots for a building site in
Eagle, but there was not one dollar in the treasury of the Seattle-
Yukon Transportation Co. to use there. On one of the lots was a
log cabin about ten feet by twelve feet and in this I opened up my
store. Butter, cream and sugar, three things most in demand, were
very short in my stock, but I was there to sell what I had and to
build a store and warehouse.

"I bought, on tick, the lumber for the frame of a warehouse
50'x100' and I had corrugated iron enough to cover it. I let a
contract for a log store 18'x 40' with two stories. It had a rough
board floor, and before Christmas the boards had shrunk till there
was more than half an inch between them.

"I succeeded in trading what gold dust we took in for government
drafts with one of the other stores who seemed to be desirous of
having a big gold dust shipment in the spring. The next year when
I had $1500 coming to me, I suggested that dry goods, shoes and
other things be purchased for me. This was done, and out of the
first money for goods sold came my principal, next the freight and
the profits were divided between me and company. The company's own
funds were put into groceries and hardware. My salary was $250 per
month and board. Miss Thompson had a boarding house where we
single agents and clerks boarded, and my sleeping accommodations
were upstairs in the store.

"The Seattle-Yukon Transportation Co. had been organized on the
discovery of the Klondike, and there was some English money
invested. They were good people to work for, and I had a good job
at good wages. We traded some with the Indians, and this was
interesting as well as profitable. They brought in furs, and sheep,
caribou and moose meat. I encouraged them in making baskets,
beaded gloves, moccasins, etc. which the tourists on the steamers
purchased.

SEATTLE-YUKON TRANSPORTATION CO. 1899
Courtesy: Blake D. Mills, Jr.

"Some Indians from the Peel River country came in one day, and their English had a Scottish accent, picked up, no doubt, from the Scottish employees of the Hudson Bay Co. If a woman or man would have $20 worth of furs, the first purchase would be $5 for tea (5 pounds), then some tobacco, a little cloth, powder, lead, etc. and then maybe some more tea. They would stay a few days or a week, and then head back to their food supply.

"The Customs Collector for Alaska wanted a building for a Customs House. Carl Johansen and I bought a lot on the waterfront and built a small office building, one story, which we rented to them for $100 per month. On the other end of the lot, we built a two story frame building which we rented to Peoples and Woodruff for a store. This was not a profitable investment, because they gave up the building after two or three years, and the Customs Service vacated after a few years too.

"There were always a few men out prospecting in the hills back of Eagle, and I knew most of them and felt sure that if anything was struck I would have a chance to get in on it. No very rich pay had yet been found near Eagle though American Creek and Seventymile had produced some gold. We were all in Alaska to make a fortune, but there was not that keenness that there is outside.

"As things settled down, we found there were too many trading stations for the amount of business. Finally there was a consolidation of the Alaska Commercial Co. and the Alaska Exploration Co. and they bought out my company. I was soon to be out of a job and wondering what I would do.

"Mr. Merriman, agent of the N.A.T.& T. Co. decided to quit and go outside and he recommended me for the place. I gave him $200 for three lots and his watch and I got the job. I enjoyed ordering the goods and figuring the costs and selling them. In the winter I would pore over the catalogs. If I could sell one single item, say a curling iron, for instance, I ordered it. The first year sales jumped from $38,000 to $45,000 and the next year to $70,000.

"While Eagle was not a legally incorporated city, we had organized. We elected a city council and I was elected mayor.

"Carl Johansen had a sawmill just below the town, and he and I had been figuring where else in Alaska we could put a sawmill to make it pay. We had been thinking of the Fortymile country, but had not decided anything. Then a Japanese man named Wada arrived from Fairbanks over the trail in the spring of 1903. When Wada told us of the new gold strike there, Johanson and I decided that this was our opportunity and moved the mill to Fairbanks. I was to manage the mill, so on December 1, 1903, I gave up my job with the N.A.T.& T. Co."

Mr. Mills remained in Fairbanks, running the sawmill until 1906. That year, his fiance Gertrude Reitze of Seattle came to Alaska and they were married July 6th in the little log church in Tanana. Later in the same year they returned to Seattle where they remained for the rest of their lives.

THE THOMPSON FAMILY

The Thompson family was one of the earliest business families in Eagle and remained in business for decades. Thirty year old Louise J. Thompson (Lulu), a school teacher from the state of Washington, arrived in Eagle July 1899 with another teacher, Miss Lois Adams, and two of her brothers. They hiked over the Chilkoot trail, built a boat and floated down the Yukon to Dawson in the spring of 1899. She said the trip was a picnic. With all of their possessions aboard and themselves comfortably housed under a tent erected on a flat boat, they had a jolly time floating with the current. The brothers enjoyed the white water and they came through the Whitehorse Rapids without any problems (Maddock, 1989). Stopping only two days in Dawson, Lulu arrived in Eagle on the 1st of July and opened a restaurant in a tent and made it pay (McLean, 1905:80). The ladies' establishment enjoyed a good reputation. They bought and served wild sheep meat whenever possible, which was a special treat for their customers.

Later they built a road house, using green logs except for the lumber that had been whipsawed to build their boat. Lulu was energetic and independent and was the postmaster from September 1900 through August 1905. Her piano and her small but well selected library indicted she was a woman of culture. She was also generous; with her Alaska savings, she bought a small farm near Seattle for her parents (McLean 1905:81).

Misses Adams and Thompson were active in the social affairs of the town, which included many dances, amateur plays, picnics, etc. Besides the successful business they operated, Miss Adams was selected as the teacher in the new city school, teaching there from 1903-1906. Miss Thompson served as the Postmistress in Eagle from September 18, 1900 through August 14, 1905, during which time the post office was located in a back room of the Alaska Commercial Store.

Lulu Thompson had raised Cora Gustin following her mother's death. After finishing high school at 16 years of age, Cora came to Eagle City to help Lulu, but was later sent back to Seattle to attend the Puget Sound University (PSU). There, at 19 years of age, she met and married Clyde Thompson, Lulu's brother, who was also attending PSU. The couple made their home in Eagle City (Thompson 1991).

After the new gold strike in Fairbanks in 1903, Lulu moved there and taught school. Later she opened a businessman's lunch room where she met Roy Maddocks and married him in 1906. The Maddocks had two sons.

At Eagle in 1906, Clyde and Cora bought Bevington's house on the corner of First and Amundsen Streets. Besides being Postmaster, Clyde had a mercantile license. That year they were expecting their second child which was delivered by a local midwife. In 1912, Clyde purchased a general merchandise store, the Eagle Trading Co. from Lt. David Henkes who had been transferred from Fort Egbert.

As the family grew, the Thompsons supplemented their food supply by growing a beautiful vegetable garden. Clyde was an excellent gardner and he shipped out some of the best potatoes. They also raised poultry and kept a cow. Thompsons also had a fox farm on the island opposite town. Little five foot tall Cora had a hard life, baking bread to sell, giving piano lessons, knitting socks and sewing all of the children's clothes, carrying water from the well house, cutting wood and raising beautiful flowers.

CORA THOMPSON & CHILDREN IN FRONT OF THEIR RESIDENCE.
Courtesy: Lucilla McCall, EHS.

Profit from the Eagle Trading Company did not increase as fast as the Thompson family did. Clyde purchased furs, Indian moccasins and handwork and extended a lot of credit to the Indians. As was the custom with the local business men, he outfitted many of the

miners as an investment which did not pay off. He was indebted to
many of his suppliers for groceries, hardware and other items he
handled (EHS Archives 1915:Thompson). The real crunch came when the
United States Post Office Inspector arrived in Eagle in 1917 and
found a shortage of funds in the post office. Thompson admitted to
the shortage and was told the post office department would not deal
too harshly with him, if he made the shortage good. Three of his
Eagle friends had already used their local property for security so
that Thompson could be bonded in 1913. Jack Hillard loaned Clyde
$5,000 to make good the shortage but Thompson's tenure with the
postal service ended in October, 1917 (EHS Archives 1917:Thompson).

These were difficult times for Cora Thompson. She was desperate to
move outside of Alaska where her children could get an education.
Clyde refused to assist with her travel, so she gave music lessons
and baked until she had enough money saved. The year before leaving, one of the traveling doctors told Cora she had tuberculosis
and she should not have anymore children. However, she was pregnant
once again before leaving Eagle.

Jack Hillard and his wife were very fond of the Thompson children.
The Hillards assisted Cora with her tickets to Seattle which cost
$370. She left Eagle on the last sternwheeler in September, 1918
with the children and all of her belongings, as she had reserva-
tions on the ill fated Canadian vessel, S.S.Sophia. Upon her
arrival in Skagway, she received word from Jack Hillard that
influenza was rampant outside and advised her to remain in Skagway
until spring. Though all of her belongings were already on board
the S.S. Sophia and were later lost when the ship went down, Cora
and the children spent the winter in Skagway upon Hillard's
recommendation (EHS Archives 1991: Thompson).

Arriving in Glendale, California with six children, pregnant and
little money, no one would rent Cora a house. In desperate need,
she called a distant relative in Pomona and after a week with them,
he quickly found them a house, just in time for the baby to be
delivered. By that time Cora's funds were really low and Jack
Hillard bought them a house. Cora, as sick as she was, weak from
childbirth and tuberculosis, was taking a correspondence course in
advanced sewing. Again in desperation, Cora called for help from
the County Welfare, so that the family would have food. Clyde
Thompson kept his word about refusing to pay any support for his
family, so it was the Los Angeles County, new neighbors and the
Hillards who supported the family (EHS Archives 1991:Thompson).

Cora, who was still nursing the baby at fifteen months, was failing
rapidly, so both she and the baby were placed in the San Fernando
Tuberculosis Sanitorium. The other children were placed in foster
homes. Cora died at the age of 38. The baby remained in the
sanitorium, but was later adopted and raised by the Hillards. Clyde
refused to allow any of the other children to be adopted; only the
baby, as he was deep in debt to the Hillards and didn't dare refuse

them (EHS Archives 1991:Thompson).

Clyde Thompson remained in Eagle. In 1929 he married Mary Angus
from Eagle Village on her death bed (she also died from tuberculosis). They had four children, Ruth, Clifford, Charles and Ethel.
After Mary's death, Anne Purdy adopted Charles and Ethel. Their
school teacher, Borghilde Henricksen, cared for Ruth and Clifford
until they were sent down river to live with Dr. and Mrs. Burke at
Fort Yukon. Later they went to Eklutna High School. In 1931, Ruth
the oldest, was 13 years old.

Clyde Thompson's third wife, Vera, was a mail order bride. She
came to Eagle late in the summer of 1933 and died the spring of
1934 of unknown causes.

Clyde continued to maintain his store, though he did little
business except buying and selling furs and selling moose hides and
Indian moccasins. Jack Hillard always said Clyde was an educated
derelict who would have been a millionaire, if he hadn't grubstaked
so many miners who never returned through Eagle, but went outside
the other way.

In 1936, Clyde and Cora's daughter Lillis Thompson spent the summer
in Eagle with her father. She helped him haul lumber while cooking
lunches and dinners for four of the local men including her father.
In 1940 Ruth Thompson returned to Eagle. February 12, 1941, Clyde
Thompson died in his sleep in Eagle.

In 1941 and 1942, Lillis and Guilbert, one of the twin boys,
returned to Eagle. During those years, Ruth and Lillis operated the
Steel Road house and were known for their good meals. Guilbert,
better known as Buster, served as Postmaster and United States
Commissioner for two years. Buster left to fight in World War II,
but returned to Alaska where he taught school in many communities
and remained after his retirement.

JESS & CATHRYNE KNIGHT
Carol Copeland

A lifetime of love and adventure began for Jess and Cathryne Knight
when they married on April 16, 1932 in Kansas City, Missouri. In
September, they packed a pannier with clothes, got on a 1917 Indian
motorcycle and took Route 66 to Vista, California where Jess's
parents and sisters lived. Jess needed a paying job, but the
country was in a severe depression. Though there were few jobs,
Jess found one cutting wood for 10 cents an hour; this was not his
idea of a good job. They needed a miracle. A letter from Alaska
containing a check for $75 came from Jess's older brother, Bill
Knight. He encouraged them to come to Circle, Alaska where he was
government radio operator.

The newlyweds packed to travel north and sailed for Seward. They
took a train to Fairbanks and were flown to Circle, arriving April
4th. Bill Knight welcomed them to the United States Radio Station
which would be their temporary home.

Circle had boomed during the gold rush. By the time the Knights
arrived, the city had returned to being a native village of
approximately 80 residents. Small log cabins lined the river bank.
Behind the cabins were dog houses, outhouses and caches. There was
a general mercantile store (Northern Commercial Company), a road
house, an Episcopal Church and the radio station.

Every day was a new adventure, but the need to earn a living had
not disappeared. Jess, with his brother Bill as financial partner,
purchased a log cabin and started a trading business. Jess supplied
his business with canned food and merchandise he purchased in
Fairbanks (162 miles away) and trucked to Circle. He also bought
traps, dogs, guns and other equipment from miners and trappers
leaving the Circle area. A profit was made on those who sold out
and left the country.

Life in Circle was not all work. Occasionally Cathryne and Jess
would drive 42 miles to Circle Hot Springs to enjoy the 'baths',
then on to the Central Roadhouse where they danced and enjoyed a
midnight supper for 50 cents a plate. The night's lodging cost
$2.00 and breakfast was $1.00 each. The hunting season began in the
fall. Caribou migrated past the Circle area by the thousands. Not
only did they hunt with the natives, but they took movies of the
hunt with their new 16mm camera.

Since Jess owned a team of dogs and wanted more income, he contracted to be a mail carrier for $40 per month plus helping his
brother trap. His mail run was from Circle to Coal Creek every two
weeks. One winter as a mail carrier was enough. It was cold
dangerous work and Jess did not like to be away from Cathryne.

In the spring of 1934, the Northern Commercial Company offered Jess
the position of manager of their Circle store. Circle was not
large enough for two trading operations and the N. C. Co. wanted to
buy the Knights out. An agreement was reached and Cathryne and

Jess moved into the big log building built before 1900 by the pioneer Yukon trader, Jack McQuesten.

To add to their income, Cathryne became the Postmistress for the Circle area. The post office was in the store building and the mail carriers operated like the pony express. The mail was relayed and mushers could arrive at any hour, day or night, depending on the weather or river conditions. Carol Lee, their first child, was born May 30th, 1935 at St. Joseph Hospital in Fairbanks. Nine days later Cathryne and her daughter were flown home to Circle.

JESS & CATHRYNE KNIGHT (1980's)
Courtesy: Eagle Historical Society

Summers were hectic. There was the store to manage. Mail was coming and going by river boat and the steamboats would arrive with tons of freight. In addition, there was a little baby to love and care for without modern conveniences. Even getting fresh clean water in Circle was a problem. River water had to set for hours before the mud would settle and ice from the ice house was not very satisfactory by late summer.

By the spring of 1937, the Knights were ready for a change. Jess resigned from the N. C. Co. They finally arrived in the states in

September, 1937, where they visited with friends and family and shared their 16mm movies and stories of their four years of adventure.

In February 1938, Jess received a telegram from the N. C. Co. offering management of their store in Eagle, Alaska, requesting him to come as soon as possible. The offer included a salary of $100 per month, a fully furnished house and an assistant which he didn't have in Circle. As a new baby would arrive soon, Jess accepted the offer and informed the company he would return to Alaska as soon as Cathryne was able to travel. William Allen Knight was born March 1, 1938 in Kansas City. On May 1st, they flew to Eagle and received a warm welcome from the local residents.

The family was escorted to the Northern Commercial Company's house, two blocks from the airstrip. To Cathryne's joy, this log house was completely furnished from sheets to silverware. There was a Kohler generator which provided electricity for the house and store where messages were sent to Fairbanks using the Morse Code. Later Jess installed a chemical toilet and bathtub in the generator shed. There was a wood stove for winter use. The City's well house was across the street so hauling water would be easy. A lovely side yard held beautiful birch trees and space for a large garden. The entire property was fenced to keep roaming horses from the garden.

When the Knights arrived in 1938, Eagle was on the decline from its bustling gold rush and army days of 1900. There was an Episcopal church and manse, a school, well house, roadhouse, custom house, several mercantile stores and the Redmen Hall. Some abandoned Fort buildings were still standing, plus an empty court house.

There was never a dull moment during those first weeks. On May 22, Jess walked up the alley to the house for lunch. Cathryne had put Billy, now almost three months old, out in the side yard for his afternoon nap. Carol had lunch and was on her way to Anne Hansen's house to play with her children. Jess had just walked in the house when they heard shots. Out the front door they flew expecting to see caribou crossing the river. Bob Steel ran out of the road-house, looked around hollered to Jess, "There goes a black bear behind your fence by the alley." Luckily the garden gate was closed, so Billy was safe. The bear scampered out the alley, cut across the court house yard and headed up the street toward Ann's. Carol was just two minutes ahead of the bear. She opened the gate to Anne's yard and did not close it. Ann was chopping wood at that moment. By now the men with the guns were chasing the bear. Anne heard all the commotion, looked up and saw the bear dash into her yard. She threw her ax at him and the frightened bear jumped the low fence and ran across the street into Frank Omo's yard where the animal was shot. The meat was distributed and the Knights had bear meat for supper.

After the river ice broke-up and the Yukon was cleared of ice, the steamboats started arriving. It took about 18 hours nonstop for the deck hands to unload the Eagle freight. Jess was back in the same hectic routine as in Circle, except Eagle was a port of entry into U.S. Territory, so everything had to go through customs.

Before Christmas, Cathryne and the school children went to the wooded hills to select a large spruce tree. They decorated the tree with colored electric lights and placed it by the front corner of their log house for all of the residents to enjoy. The 'old timers' were thrilled to see the first Christmas tree with electric lights, thanks to the generator. Then came the annual Christmas Eve party at the Redmen Lodge. The big tree at the hall was decorated and had piles of presents under it. The six school children presented a program, after which Santa arrived with a pack on his back and gave presents to all the excited children. Many of the miners had also come to town for the celebration. After all the presents were opened, the dancing began. A supper of sandwiches, hand cranked ice cream, cookies and coffee was served after midnight. Carol finally fell asleep on a bench with a ham sandwich in one hand and a new doll in the other. The dance ended at 3 a.m. and the Knights took their sleeping children home. The temperature was minus 40 degrees.

Home chores kept Cathryne on the go from early morning to late in the evening. She had to haul water from across the street, keep the stoves full of wood, empty the night slop pail, fill the gasoline lamps (they didn't always use the generator), cook meals on the wood range, bake bread and pack snow into copper boilers for soft water as she preferred to melt snow for wash water, in addition to being a loving, caring mother.

Carol was six years old May 30, 1941 and the Knights were concerned about school. There were not enough children in the town of Eagle and no teacher was scheduled. Cathryne wrote her good friend, Bessie Doan in Central of their need for a teacher. School started in September.

December 7, 1941 - Pearl Harbor., Fear pierced the hearts of all Americans, especially Alaskans, as Alaska was much too close to Japan. The Knights spent December 1941 and all winter of 1942 with one ear tuned to the radio. The Knights were in a dilemma. Should they stay in Eagle or return to Kansas City as soon as possible? Should they send their children to Cathryne's mother? They decided to stay in Eagle. The residents began supporting the war effort; the young men joined the army while the women knitted and made bandages. Jess was required to make six weather reports each day, beginning at 5:30 a.m. for the military and commercial pilots. This information was sent to Fairbanks using the Morse Code. Cathryne ceased writing as many letters because they were now being censored.

As the fall of 1942 approached, the Knights were again faced with the problem of education for Carol. Joe and Lou White were the government teachers at the native village three miles from Eagle. The Knights enjoyed their friendship and the Whites had a son a year older than Carol. It was decided that Carol would attend the second grade at the village school. During the warm fall days, she rode her bike. When it became colder, Jess drove her in their car until snow closed the road. When it became extremely cold, Carol boarded with the Whites. Jess and Cathryne walked to the village often to visit and take Carol clean clothes.

By June 1943, it was time for a change. The Knights were deeply concerned about the school problem and frightened by the war. Jess resigned from the N.C. Co. and they were all (family, trunks and car) on the late June steamboat headed for Circle. From there they drove to Fairbanks where Jess got a government job as a welder. This job paid well so the Knights stayed in Fairbanks until October 1944 when they returned to Kansas City.

In Missouri Jess worked as a brakeman for the southern Pacific Railroad which kept him away from his family too much. When the telegram arrived from the N. C. Co.'s home office in Seattle offering him the management of the Eagle store again, his spirits soared. After consulting with Cathryne, he accepted the offer; they were more than ready for the peaceful life in Eagle. They had had enough of crowds, food shortages and the noisy, dirty cities.

On a beautiful morning in early September, the Knights flew to Eagle in a small plane. Again they were greeted at the airstrip; this time with faces of people they knew and loved. They were home again by the Yukon River.

There had been changes in Eagle during their absence. The population of Eagle had dropped to an all time low with only 60 residents, but many dear friends were still living there. The road- house was closed so the Redmen Hall and the Episcopal Church were now the only centers for Eagle's social and religious life.

Airplanes were making regular stops and all mail and considerable freight were being flown into Eagle. Jess had access to a vehicle called a 'snowmobile.' This was a truck that looked like a pickup but had wide tracks which enabled it to go over the snow. One of Jess's many jobs was to attach a roller to this vehicle and roll or pack the landing strip for the airplanes. A real treat for the children was to hitch a ride on coaster sleds while Jess rolled the field. Jess would attach long ropes from the vehicle to the sleds. This was great fun and resulted in planned collisions, tangled ropes and sleds and a few bruises.

In June 1946, Jess bought Jack Hillard's old 1926 Oakland for transportation to deliver supplies to the natives at Eagle Village and to go on fishing and hunting trips. The gravel Taylor Highway now extended 30 miles out of Eagle. A year later, Billy learned to drive and was delivering groceries to Eagle Village when he was ten years old.

During September, Jess decided to treat Cathryne and the children to a hunting trip. Supplies were packed in the old Oakland and the Knights drove to American Summit, 22 miles from Eagle, where they set up camp. The days were beautiful with the hills covered with red moss and the bushes in full color. There were lots of cranberries and some late blueberries. The Knights picked berries, roamed the hills, fed the camp robbers and waited.

Morning came. They awakened to the clicking noise of hooves moving over the small rocks and moss, the chomping as the caribou grazed and the constant belly grunts all caribou make. They were surrounded by caribou. For some time the family just sat and watched the animals graze. Jess looked over the herd, chose the animal he wanted for meat, took a position, raised his .30-06 rifle and shot. Down went the animal. Now the work began, cleaning and quartering the caribou. The heart, liver and tongue were removed. Jess attached a rope to each leg and Carol and Billy helped pull the meat, hair side down, over the moss to the side of the car. Cathryne started a camp fire on that crisp fall morning and they enjoyed hot tea and blueberry pancakes. Later Jess broke camp, loaded their supplies in the car and tied the meat on top. They returned to town refreshed by the few days spent on American Summit and very pleased to have a supply of fresh meat and berries.

School started September 16, 1947. During the winter months, light was limited to six to ten hours, depending on the month, but that did not curtail any outdoor fun. The children played in the dark and in the moonlight; they were always outdoors snow-tunneling, enjoying their coaster sleds and toboggans, especially if a sled dog was available to pull them. There was also ice skating on the overflow on Mission Creek or just sliding on the seat of your pants. Cathryne enjoyed playing outdoors with her children.

Jess and Cathryne were becoming painfully aware that they had to leave Eagle. School would not open in the Fall. There was not enough business for two mercantile stores to be profitable, so Jess gave the N. C. Co. notice effective in late August. In July, he began the serious business of constructing a raft for his family and the car. His plan was to raft down river to Circle and drive the Alcan Highway to Kansas City. So, while the children played during those long sunny Alaskan days, swimming in the Pete Lundeen slough, climbing the bluff, fishing, bike riding and picnicking, Cathryne began packing the steamer trunks while Jess worked on the raft.

On July 12th, 1947, Jess put the car on the construction of timber and 18 empty sealed gas drums for floats and launched the raft. It did not sink! Jess's raft was the talk of the town for days. The project finally took shape with nine gas drums welded together on each side, a lumber base, the car on the base, and paddle wheels on the tires made from the end boards of gas boxes. It was all engineered so Jess could use car power to propel the raft down river. Then he constructed long river oars to maneuver the raft right or left. A small boat was tied to the raft in case of disaster. The family departed on August 14th, arriving in Circle on August 20th. Eddie O'Leary used his 'cat' to get the car off the raft and up the river-bank. What a relief for Jess; they had made it without any mishaps! They continued their trip on to the states, arriving in Kansas City September 14th.

Jess went to work as a clerk for the A. & P. grocery. Jess had

spent too many years being a manager to be happy as a clerk. For
a third time, a 'summons' came from the N. C. Co. This time they

JESS KNIGHT FAMILY RAFTING FROM EAGLE
TO CIRCLE IN 1947 WITH 1926 OAKLAND CAR.
Courtesy: Harold Uvie, EHS

wanted Jess to go to Fort Yukon, the largest native village on the
Yukon River to manage the N. C. store. This offer was for 'big
money', and Jess said, "Yes," even though it meant leaving Carol
and Billy with their grandmother.

Their Fort Yukon sojourn was to be brief, just two years. In the
spring of 1949, they experienced the worst flood of their lives.
Fort Yukon was a native village and they missed white people. Jess
resigned during the summer of 1950.

Returning to Kansas City, the Knights purchased a small neighbor-
hood grocery store. The entire family worked to make it profitable,
but soon business fell off; big chain stores were taking business
from the 'Ma and Pa' groceries. The store was closed and auctioned
off in 1963. Jess took some odd jobs, mainly trucking across the
country.

Something was missing.......Alaska. So when a desperate call came
from Florence Biederman in the late spring of 1967, their destiny
was sealed. Florence begged them to return to Eagle and manage her

44

father's store as Horace Biederman was very ill with heart disease. Preparations were made to drive to Eagle and off they drove in early July never realizing they would be residents of Alaska until December 1988.

Jess and Cathryne arrived in Eagle on August 2nd exhausted and covered with dust from the Alcan Highway. The store was a mess. There were no supplies, not even eggs, bread or a sack of potatoes; only some pancake mix was to be found on the shelves.

By August 15th, the store had been scrubbed and the shelves were stocked. Jess had bought a lot of freight, all on credit. There wasn't much trade with the local white people (about 40) as they trucked in their own supplies to supplement their productive gardens. The tourists stopped to buy gasoline.

A big problem for the Biederman store was cash flow; no money to buy supplies. In the old N. C. days, men left money at the store (on deposit like a bank), so there were times the safe held thousands of dollars. There was no money now and no wages for the Knights. Jess talked to Amund Hagen, an old timer, about this situation. Amund went home and returned with several thousand dollars for Jess to have on deposit and from which to draw. Jess' good reputation from his N. C. days paid off. Jess was trying hard to save the store, but the entire operation was in the red. On February 24, 1968 sad news was received; Horace Biederman had died. Florence, who now owned the store, asked the Knights to continue to work for her.

By 1972, after three and one-half years of hard work and superb management, the Biederman store was profitable. Jess was proud of the report he sent to Florence. For the first time Cathryne and Jess were talking of retirement. They had purchased the old N. C. store building and were negotiating the purchase of the N. C. Warehouse. They finally had property on the river front for their retirement living. Jess left in early March to drive to Kansas City for their furniture and personal supplies while Cathryne operated the store. He returned to Eagle on May 10th.

Cathryne and Jess were tired and it was time to close the shop. The Knights planned to retire in June. Jess began the serious work of creating an apartment in back of the old log N. C. store which had been built in 1899. On a day in early June 1974, Cathryne and Jess locked the store door, made the last business entry in the books and opened a new door to retirement on the river front. Cathryne would be 62 years old and Jess would soon be 65. They so loved living on the banks of the Yukon River. Jess became the unofficial greeter to all of the tourists admiring the river while Cathryn hosted their three grandsons plus Jess' new friends during the summer months. Winters found them traveling, visiting loved ones and enjoying their Kansas City home. However, Jess and Cathryne were forced to leave their retirement home in Eagle due to poor health in 1988. Jess passed away in Dec. 1992 in Kansas City and Cathryn in 1996.

ANNA MALM
1844-1932

One of the smallest businesses in early Eagle, could have been Anna
Malm's Arctic Laundry. It was a welcomed addition to the community.

Anna and her husband, Abe, were from Finland. Though they spoke
little English, they decided to seek their fortune in the northern
gold fields, mushing in over the Chilkoot trail. Though Anna was
54 years old at that time, she packed her load on her back the same
as her husband, who was 19 years younger. Anna had raised Abe and
then married him.

Arriving in Eagle in 1898, they squatted on a city lot and lived in
a tent while they built a cabin. Abe prospected out on the creeks
and while he was gone, he instructed his wife to hold the fort and
not to let anyone step foot on their ground, as town lot jumping
was common practice. "One day when Anna was alone, two men appeared
and ordered her off, claiming the ground was theirs by some prior
right. She spoke but little English and barely understood them,
but the usually mild-mannered little lady was sailing under orders.
She opened up and fairly deluged the two trespassers with such a
flowing flood of Finnish that she almost swept them over the river
bank into the Yukon" (Davis, 1933).

The Malm's were a hard working couple. Besides his prospecting, Abe
worked as a laborer in town; he had filed claims on the Seventymile River as well as mining with Bob Murray on the Green Bench of
American Creek. Anna not only operated her laundry, but also
cleaned the school, city hall, the well-house, church, and IOOR
lodge. Abe was also active in community affairs; he served on the
city council as an election Judge, worked as the Chief of Police
and Superintendent of a quarantine camp and was an active member of
the Improved Order of Redmen. The young folks made Abe and Anna
learn to dance, and they got to be pretty good dancers.

In 1910 Abe became ill and it was suspected he had cancer. The town
folks took up a collection and sent him to Seattle during the
summer for medical attention. The cancer in his duodenum had
spread too far to treat, so Abe returned to Eagle. On December 7,
1913, Abe died and was buried by the Improved Order of Redmen in
the Eagle cemetery.

After Abe's death, Anna sent for her sister in Finland to come to
Eagle to live with her. Marie arrived in 1920. Though Anna was
very friendly and talkative, Marie was quieter, and spoke even less
English. She only said yes or no to visitors. The sisters lived a
quiet life, continuing to support themselves by their laundry
business. They were both marvelous cooks and would do anything for
people, giving them angel food cakes, etc. They knitted and
crocheted on everything, even their underwear.

ANNA MALM WITH HER SISTER, MARIE,
HAULING WATER FROM THE CITY WELLHOUSE
Courtesy: Borghilde Hanson, EHS

Anna cooked at various mining camps. One year she spent the summer
at Crooked Creek. At the age of 82, Mrs. Malm walked in from the
Seventymile River in one day (26 miles). It had been raining and
the mud was ankle deep. She had one summit to cross. When questioned about her trip after reaching home, she admitted to being a
little tired.

Sister Marie developed cancer of the duodenum in 1932 and went to
the Fort Yukon Hospital for treatment. When she returned to Eagle,
Anna took care of her. Anna had had pneumonia, but was improving
when her sister died in October. Anna told them not to close the
grave; within 48 hours she too was dead. The sisters were buried in
a common grave at the Eagle Cemetery. Anna was 87 years old, and
was active to the end. She had lived in Eagle 34 years.

CHAPTER 5

GOLD MINING

The presence of gold in the upper Yukon area had been obvious since the first European explorations and was well known to the Indians. The Indians found the gold useless as it provided neither food nor warmth, and the first white men to reach the area were sent to establish trading posts and to purchase furs. In 1850 Robert Campbell was aware of the gold around Fort Selkirk and the Reverend Robert McDonald had found gold on Birch Creek, but Campbell's primary interest was in exploration and the fur trade and McDonald's was in missionary work.

George Holt is credited with being the first man to send gold out of Alaska - two small nuggets obtained from a Tanana Indian. Prospectors followed within a year or two. After the big California gold strike, prospectors had been working their way north from California through British Columbia, Northwest Territories, and Souteast Alaska at various gold fields, keeping their ears open for other lucrative areas. The great unknown valley of the Yukon, having never been glaciated, left the gold where it laid in the richest placer streams ever discovered in the world, as it had not been plucked up and scattered by overriding ice. Nearly all the prospectors found color at some point, but always in small amounts.

It wasn't until 1886 that a major strike was made on the Fortymile River and miners rushed into the area. Harry Madison and Howard Franklin had lined their boat twenty-three miles up the Fortymile River into American territory and discovered a large quantity of coarse gold - the first rich placer on the Yukon. By 1887 pay dirt was also found on other tributaries of the Fortymile River. During that year more than 200 men went over the divide to that area and approximately $250,000 in gold was taken out during the season.

These gold discoveries lured more prospectors into the country. With the rising population, commerce was expanded and sternwheelers were built to use on the Yukon River. The culmination of the gold fever was the discovery of fabulous amounts of the yellow metal on the side streams of the Klondike River. Robert Henderson made the original find on Bonanza Creek in the summer of 1896. News of this strike left most of the other mining areas deserted as the miners hurried to establish their claims. The panning was so rich that the most valuable ground was claimed before news of the big strike reached the outside world.

Men and women swarmed to the Klondike after the word of the gold strike reached them. Few were physically or mentally fit for the life of a prospector in the far north. They were desperate people on a great search, some still suffering from the results of the depression. Many were immigrants who had poured out of Europe. The

Unfortunately, with most of the rich ground on the Klondike having already been claimed before 1898, the thousands of late comers had a choice of either working as a laborer on another man's claim, or moving down the river to prospect other creeks. The 10% royalty charged on all the gold taken out of the Canadian Territory so upset some of the miners that they chose to move on to Alaska.

Small gold discoveries had been found on American Creek in 1894 (Grumman 1980:15) and on Mission Creek in 1895 (Osgood 1971:8). Settling near the mouth of Mission Creek in 1897, a group formed a settlement that they named Eagle City. It became a roaring mining camp, but the gold deposits were not extensive or exceptionally rich and the cost of extraction was high. About a thousand people wintered in Eagle the first year, but like the winter's snow, the population melted away; the large majority moved on looking for richer gold strikes.

The richest ground in the Eagle area was found on American Creek, Fortymile River and Seventymile River. One naive miner came into the Fortymile country to strike it rich, bringing only a hacksaw with him. He said he only intended to saw a chunk of gold off the mother lode; he didn't need a lot. Some of the miners made their stake, sold out and left, while others remained in the Eagle District for the rest of their lives. To many it was the thrill of the hunt for gold as they continued their prospecting. Large mining companies purchased some of the working claims, invested in dredges and other large equipment and lost their investor's money. The companies apparently made their money on Wall Street from gullible gold investors. The old timers said more money was poured into these areas than was ever taken out. Some claimed that for every dollar in gold taken out of the Fortymile area, five dollars had been brought in to develop the mining.

There was a certain lure to the independent life of a miner that attracted many individuals. Some would find a fair placer mining site and work it for a lifetime. They usually lived in a small fourteen-foot square cabin furnished with a stove, bunk, table and a couple of stools. The miner's diet was often poor, unless they had fresh meat, as the diet was heavy on white flour and sugar. One who was a food crank and raised a large garden lived to be over a hundred years old.

The work these men did was amazing. They spent the cold winter months prospecting by digging holes down to bedrock. Every inch of the frozen ground had to be thawed. Prospectors would burn fires all night in numerous holes, dig out the depth of thawed ground the next morning, usually about eight inches of soil or twelve inches of gravel and go through the same routine the next day. After the holes reached a depth where they couldn't throw the dirt out with a shovel, they built a windlass and used buckets. Once down to bedrock, they would dig along the creekbed, haul the ore through untimbered tunnels, raise it through shafts and dump it at the surface. It was sixty degrees below at the surface and a cozy thirty-three above in the tunnels.

Tunneling along the bedrock was called drift mining, one of the most difficult and dangerous kinds of mining. Sluicing started on all the soil brought up from the tunnel when the spring thaw came. If the clean-up showed good pay dirt, the miner then proceeded during the summer months to remove the top soil to get down to the bedrock to retrieve the gold. Unfortunately the spring thaw also brought instant floods and frequent cave-ins. Many a miner lies at the bottom of Alaska's drift mines.

C.J.Berry was prospecting in the Dawson area by the fire thawing method, when he got the idea that steam would be a faster method to thaw the ground. He tried it using his gun barrel secured to the end of a steam hose; it worked so well that steam points became a popular technique for which Berry is credited. Two miners could hand carry a small steam boiler to their prospecting site. Using the steam points was a much faster and more efficient method of thawing the ground, going down about six feet a day. This was usually a two man job.

Water is essential for placer mining. When water was inadequate, miners hand dug long ditches, sometimes ten miles long, and built wooden flumes as long as 7,000 feet, made from handwhip sawed lumber. One ingenious miner built a water driven sawmill over the creek to saw the necessary lumber; it took hours to cut one board. On some creeks in narrow canyons, the miners built boom dams, using the pressure of the water from the dam to strip the dirt and debris off the bedrock or sluice out the paydirt. All were dependent upon rain water; long dry periods halted their mining. Later, hydraulic mining was successful in using water pressure from hoses to remove the top soil. Water was the cheapest method to make an open cut in the ground.

The world-wide depression of the gold-mining industry in 1919 had a great effect on Alaska. Going off the gold standard in 1932, raised the price of gold from $16 an ounce to $35. Later when bull- dozers were used, it was the oil companies and equipment dealers who got the most, if not all, of the gold. When gold was worth $35 an ounce, one had to have ground worth a dollar per cubic yard to pay for the operation of a D8 cat. Before 1941, cat operators were paid $300 a month, while the other workers made $5 a day plus board, working ten hour days, seven days a week. The cook was paid $200 a month, which averaged about fifty cents an hour. Gold mining was closed down during World War II due to gasoline rationing, as the mining areas were now dependent upon machinery to operate. In the 1980's a second gold rush was experienced when the price of gold soared to over $800 an ounce; most of these miners reworked the old mining claims. Recreational mining with small hand dredges became popular.

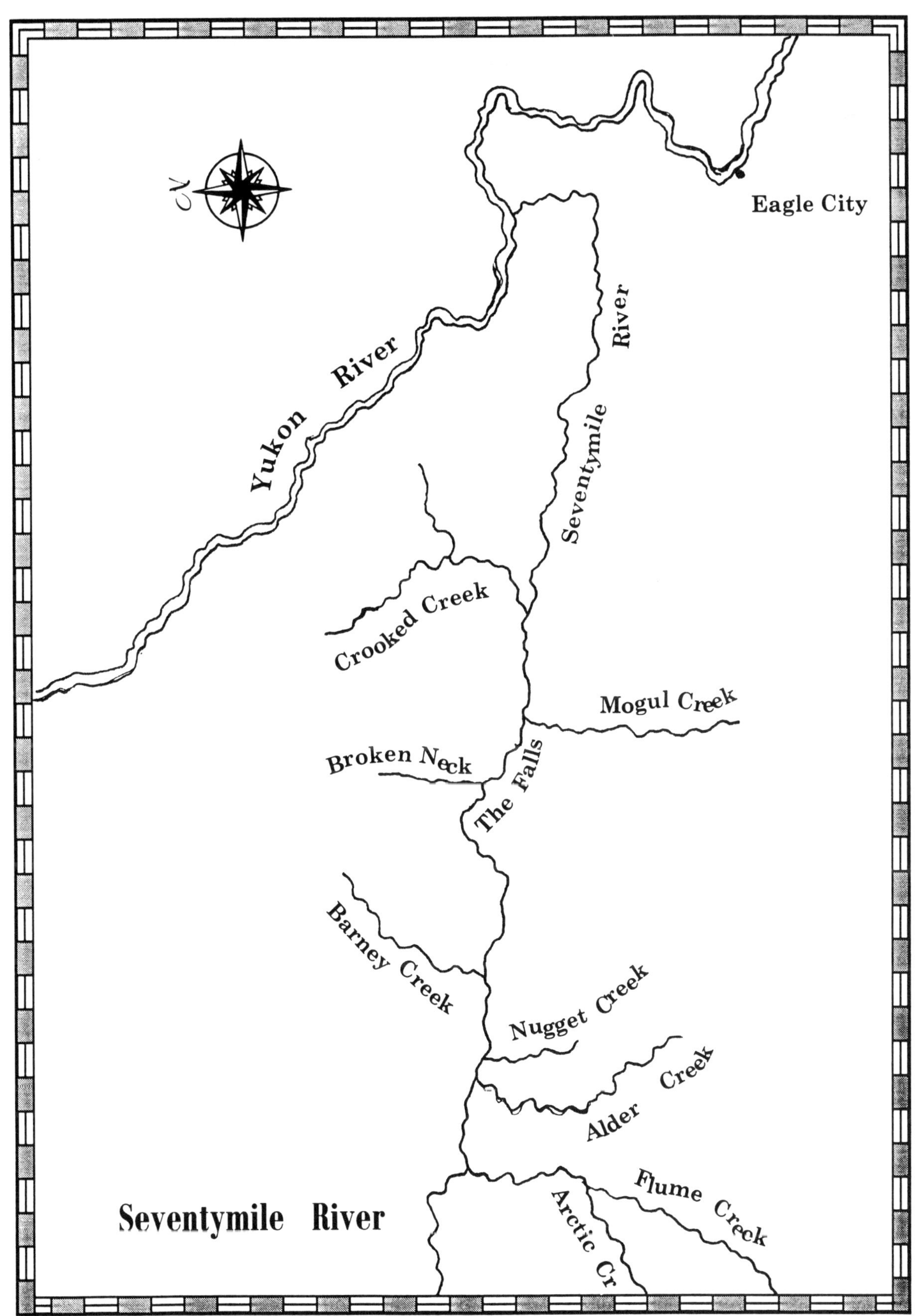

Eagle City
Yukon River
Seventymile River
Crooked Creek
Mogul Creek
Broken Neck
The Falls
Barney Creek
Nugget Creek
Alder Creek
Flume Creek
Arctic Cr
Seventymile River

ARTHUR FROELICH
1862-1932

One of the most persistent gold miners on the Seventymile River was
Arthur Froelich. He arrived in the Eagle Jurisdiction in June of
1895, and started mining on the Seventymile River in 1898, first on
Arctic Tributary. Later he mined on Flume Creek where he found
large pieces of gold, though not many. His German friend, Hermann
Kummer, talked him into joining him at Crooked Creek in 1905, where
he mined until his death in 1932.

Froelich was born on June 17, 1862 in Berlin, Germany. He was
caught up in the great migration that poured out of Europe during
the 19th century. Though Froelich's family remained in Germany, he
kept in close touch with his mother and sisters, often sending them
money. He dreamed of returning home for a visit, but the dream was
never fulfilled.

ARTHUR FROELICH
Courtesy: Eagle Historical Society

The life of Arthur Froelich's mining on the Seventymile River is well documented as he faithfully kept a diary, with at least a line or two each day. Many of the old timers kept diaries, not only to document their activities, but mainly to keep track of the days in the week and month, so that they wouldn't miss going into town for the holidays and special events. Froelich was an amateur photographer who developed and printed his own film, so there is also an excellent visual record of his activities.

George Matlock was Froelich's partner in 1903. In February they prospected full time. They recorded the number of pans of dirt removed from each hole daily. They ranged from 15 to 140. They noted that the weather was so cold the quick silver froze. It freezes at minus forty degrees. Early in the spring, they took their meat into town to sell and returned with 500 pounds of supplies. They had to do a lot of backtracking to get all of the supplies to their camp, even though both men were large and strong and carried heavy packs. Back at camp, they put up a saw pit close to the source of trees and began sawing lumber with whipsaws. They built a poling boat with their newly sawed lumber.

By the middle of May, they were mining seriously on the Arctic tributary. They built a boom dam, dug a ditch to get the water to the dam, made sluice boxes and started stripping the creek down to bedrock with a shovel and strong back. Once to bedrock, they began shoveling the dirt into the sluice boxes for the clean up. They never lacked for company as their neighboring miners often stopped in for a visit and to borrow supplies. Froelich and Matlock also traveled up and down the river visiting others, making trips to the Falls to fish for grayling, hauling bark for their cabin roof. They spent their day of rest cooking, baking (bread, pies and doughnuts were their favorites), washing and mending clothes and cleaning their cabin.

Mining during the summer of 1904 was productive, so Matlock and Froelich made a trip into Eagle to record their claims. At the end of the season they divided their gold dust and Froelich's share was worth $2177. In September, Froelich went to Eagle, caught a sternwheeler and went out to the states for the winter where he visited his two nephews living on the east coast.

Froelich returned to Alaska, docking at Valdez on March 12, 1905. From there he walked to Eagle with his dog, a sled and 150 pounds of gear. It took him three weeks to reach his destination. He was on the trail each day from 5 a.m. to 5 p.m., often spending the night out in a tent. He followed the mail trail via Copper Center, Gakona, Chistochena, Tanana Crossing, Fortymile river and on to Eagle. He rested two days, visiting and answering his letters and returned to his mining digs on Arctic Creek, which took him twelve hours due to the heavy spring snow.

Froelich resumed his partnership with Matlock. They sawed lumber for five days, built a log cabin and started their garden, flowers as well as vegetables. By May 23rd, they started working on their dump dam in the creek and putting together the sluice boxes, making it possible to start shoveling in the first of June.

On the days that the water was too low in their creeks to mine, due to lack of rain, the miners would prospect other areas or ground sluice on their upper bar out in the Seventymile River. They also used that dead time to go hunting. Getting an early bear or caribou would take days to pack in the meat. Trips would be made into Eagle to pack meat in and supplies out. At times they borrowed a neighbor's mule for the summer trips.

After supper and a full day of shoveling, Froelich would often walk down to Nimrod's cabin on Flume Creek. The miners all visited back and forth from Broken Neck, the Falls, Flume Creek, Crooked Creek, Nugget Bar, Barney, Arctic, Yellowstone and Alder Creeks, often spending the night enroute to town or while hunting. They were close friends and Froelich often referred to "The Gang" and their activities. They included Froelich, Kummer, Matlock, John Pierson, Nimrod Robertson, Axel Johnson, Charlie Martin, Bert Bryant, Charlie Yost, Harry Mason, the Hudson brothers, Bill Ziller, the Carlson brothers and others as they came and went out on the creek. Six of these miners purchased and shared a cabin in Eagle which they used during their visits to town. They also shared meat, home brew, borrowed dogs, mules, magazines, groceries and money as needed.

The miners not only led an active social live, but were physically active all year long. Cold weather did not hold them down. Many lived in tents while they were trapping, hunting and prospecting. The temperatures often dropped to fifty and sixty below zero. Winters were preferred to the warm summer days which brought hordes of mosquitos.

After dividing the summers take of gold dust with Matlock in the fall of 1905, Froelich closed a bargain to go into partnership with Hermann Kummer on Crooked Creek. Thus a new chapter of Froelich's life began when he started moving his cherished belongings down river. Froelich spent 27 years mining on Crooked Creek where the partners built a large establishment. This included two log cabins, mule barn, water driven sawmill, drying shed for their sawed lumber, caches, meat house and meat tunnel to store fresh meat and other perishables. They also kept a large garden.

Mining was hard work on the rocky Crooked Creek, as the rocks had to be removed to reach the gold bearing bedrock. They used water pressure from their boom dams to remove some, but many had to be moved manually. Life each summer consisted of building and repairing boom dams, digging and repairing ditches to divert water where it was needed, building sluice boxes and then long hours of shoveling the gold bearing sands into the boxes. When they had

plenty of rain and water in the ditches, the boom dam would dump as
many as two to six times a day. During that time, the men worked
in shifts around the clock and often hired extra help. During the
first ten years on Crooked Creek, Froelich and Kummer estimated
they had taken out about $10,000 to $12,000 in gold, which averaged
about $600 per man per year. From that they had to pay for their
living expenses, equipment and their extra workers.

SLUICING ON CROOKED CREEK
Courtesy: Eagle Historical Society

When the creek water was too low to work, the men made trips into
Eagle, went hunting, gathered firewood and cut and hauled in hay
from the farm. In August they picked blueberies and made wine, in
addition to their ever present home brewed beer.

Their hunting took them to Charlie River, up Arctic Dome and over
to Glacier Peaks. One fall they saw a brown bear, so they went to
check out the bear hole, but found no bear. When they got home,
they found the bear had visited them. It had gotten all of their
meat and raised hell with their cabin. In the fall they would get
nice fat moose, which they stored in their meat tunnel. Froelich
made special trips to bring in the moose head to make head cheese.

Winters were spent trapping, prospecting and always on the lookout for stands of timber suitable for saw logs. There were occasional breaks in their routine. One summer their mining neighbor, Bill Ziller, broke his leg. Mining was shut down and they all went after him in their poling boat to take him into Eagle. By traveling all night, they got him into town the next morning. It took them thirteen hours to return as they had to pole the boat all the way up the Seventymile River.

In 1910, four mining claims on the lower part of Crooked Creek were for sale. It was reported to be good ground. Charlie Ott and John Scheele, store operators in Eagle bought them. They quit claimed their shares to each other, making all seven claims joint property. Arthur Froelich was the manager of the work. They installed a hydraulic plant which Ott and Scheele financed. First they dug a new mile-long water ditch as they needed much more water. The hydraulic plant was laid on the ground in 1917 and was in use from 1918 until the fall of 1932.

HYDRAULIC MINING ON CROOKED CREEK
Courtesy: Eagle Historical Society

As they worked up the creek, the water pressure became less. In 1925 they had to dig a new ditch over 1.5 miles long, higher on the hillside. This was an expensive project; they later found that the ditch passed through an ice lense. The hill kept sliding down into the ditch blocking it, requiring many hours to keep it open.

In 1925, John Scheele left Eagle with his family, so Ott and Scheele paid a laborer to work in his place each summer. Hermann Kummer married his childhood sweetheart in 1929 and left Eagle. He had to pay a man to take his place.

In 1927 Froelich's health started to deteriorate. He told his friends that he had to urinate frequently, but they thought he just had a cold. By June 1933, he was in bad shape. In July he flew into Fairbanks and went to the hospital for his bladder problem. The doctors told him he needed an operation and advised him to go out to the states as they couldn't perform the surgery in Fairbanks. His friend Kummer wrote for him to join them in Michigan where he could stay and get the necessary treatment. Froelich considered going out the next spring.

In the meantime, Froelich returned to Eagle in September when it was cold and raining. All winter long his condition became worse, requiring catheters and urinal bags. He stayed out on the creek taking care of himself. He was home alone when he died March 26, 1932. Froelich was buried in the Eagle Cemetery on March 31st with a large funeral held by the Improved Order of Redmen. His friend, Bert Bryant wrote, "Froelich was a good neighbor - a fine man, loyal and honest. The latch string always hung outside his cabin door and all were welcome. That class of people are fast disappearing."

Charlie Ott was appointed Administrator of Froelich's estate and he made contact with Froelich's three widowed sisters in Germany. His total estate was appraised at $1040.64.

John Scheele returned to Alaska to work the Crooked Creek claims in 1932, but it did not pay expenses. The creek was not worked in 1933, but required annual assessment work to hold the claims. Ott tried to interest local miners in buying the claims, but money was scarce and no one was interested. Ott was in no shape to do hard work as he was 62 years old and bothered with a kidney problem; Scheele was 65 years old and had lost much in the depression and Kummer was 76 years old. The hydraulic plant had been used 16 years and was getting obsolete. The log cabins were 20 years old and needed much repair. The mining at Crooked Creek had never paid off for the partners and they were all anxious to quit the whole thing.

The few old men that lived around Eagle in 1933 had no funds, so in order to save the ground from being jumped by some other party, Ott leased all of the ground to A. L. Hagen for a period of seven years at 15% royalty, the year of 1934 to be free, with an option to buy all the ground and equipment for $3500. Through this arrangement Ott was able to send Froelich's sisters $100 to $150 each year through the German Consulate in Seattle, Washington.

GEORGE MATLOCK
1860-1933

George Matlock was a well known character among Eagle's old timers. He was a large, heavy set man whom they called the last of the mountain men and buffalo hunters. Many remember him as a happy-go-lucky and colorful guy. They liked him.

George's parents, Aaron and Sarah Matlock were born in New Jersey. They lived there until 1857, when they moved to Tipton, Iowa to join Sarah's parents. The Matlock's had six children. George, born September 21, 1860 at Tipton, Iowa was the next to youngest. After their mother died July 20, 1868, the family was broken up. Nine year old George went to live with the family of a young farmer named Thomas Moore.

George was 17 years old when he left the farm and started across the plains, down through the Dakotas and Montana. He later continued on to British Columbia. Using bulls, he used to pull stumps where Vancouver now stands. He went to Alaska in 1880, stopping at the Treadwell Mine in Douglas. When gold was discovered on the Fortymile in 1886, he went up there, ten years before Dawson existed. (EHS Archives 1986: Matlock). Besides Fortymile, George was in Eagle, Circle, Dawson and Fairbanks.

Matlock had numerous mining partners, one of them being Arthur Harper. He helped Jack McQuesten construct trading posts in Circle City and Nation. Another of his friends, Frank Buteau, wrote at length about their experiences (Heller 1967:96). "I spent the winter of 1886 at Fortymile and in the spring we started up the river to our claims. Among the miners were two men named George Matlock and Pete McDonald. During the summer of 1889, those two went down the Yukon as far as Nulato, and each came back to Franklin Gulch with a native wife."

"During the summer of 1889, the Alaska Commercial Company built a steamer called the Arctic. They loaded it with grub and started up river from their post at St. Michael. The boat struck a rock or a snag, completely destroying all of the provisions. The Alaska Commercial company sent word for the miners to go down to St. Michael for the winter, as they would not be able to get any grub up the river that fall. We got the news at Franklin Gulch on October 7th. We didn't want to go down to St. Michael as we had to whipsaw lumber and build one-half mile of flume for our new claim. We decided to winter in the Fortymile District, just making the best of what we had. Our food supply was very low, but we killed forty caribou which served as our main food. Matlock and McDonald and their wives had two sacks of flour, a few beans and a few pounds of dry fruit between them and all of those were quite moldy. They had no butter and it was during this time we learned from the native women how to make 'bone butter'."

Buteau continued, "That fall, fifteen of us made a fish trap and caught about a ton and a half of fish, so everybody had greyling for the winter. None of the miners in the Fortymile district ever

58

got ric $500 to $1500 was considered a good year's work. $3000
was the most I knew of anybody making during a year."

Buteau also recalled that a large number of miners spent the winter
of 1893-94 at the town of Fortymile. "A few men were gathered
together one evening for a social talk when trouble broke out among
them. Washburn, in whose cabin the men had gathered, became angry
at Matlock and stabbed him in the back. Matlock retaliated by
going to his cabin, secured his gun and went back to Washburn's
cabin. There being a light in the cabin, Matlock fired at him, not
with intent to kill, but to even up the score by inflicting a flesh
wound. Washburn was struck in the thigh, and both he and Matlock
had to be nursed back to good health. Later on they 'buried the
hatchet', shook hands and became friends again."

The winter up the Fortymile with Frank Buteau, was not the only
experience Matlock had without provisions. He related, "One winter
I had a partner named Nelson. Supplies were short at Fortymile.
In late August, we bought tea, 10 pounds flour and half a sack of
rutabagas. We had four dogs and each of us had a native woman. We
went up the river and got four fat moose. Before Christmas we were
hunting again, as we had to feed the dogs and ourselves. We didn't
feel satisfied on our diet, so we followed some Ketchumstock
Indians and watched what they ate   We learned to boil a pot of
water and drop chunks of meat into it, boiling only 15 to 20
minutes until you could cut the meat with a knife, still a little
red. We started cooking our meat the same way and we were always
satisfied. I came out that spring weighing 200# with $1,000 in
gold from rocking on the bars." (EHS Archives 1976:Matlock).

During his years on the Fortymile River, Matlock had native wives.
A fellow prospector recalled, "One year George had a native woman
from Ketchumstock named Maggie. George got mad at her one year and
went to Dawson. There he married a white woman, but after she
died, he returned to Maggie. George was quite a prospector in his
day. He made a lot of money in Dawson. He thought there was no end
to the money and spent it like water. He said he had no regrets,
just wished he had a little more of it later." (EHS Archives
1976:Matlock).

Billy Mitchell knew Matlock in the north and later met him in
Seattle in July 1901 (Mitchell 1953). He wrote, "A huge, shaggy
man in tattered, dirty buckskin shirt and pants strode into the
dining room of the Rainier Grand Hotel. All talk stopped and
waiters converged on him. Thrusting them aside as if merely
slapping at mosquitos, the giant surveyed the room. With plenty of
empty tables, he marched straight over to my table and seated
himself with a polite nod, 'All right with you pardner?' he asked."

"Matlock had just arrived from years in the interior of Alaska. He
had never seen an electric light, a street car or a large building.

He jerked out a heavy poke of gold dust, bounced it on the table and shouted to the waiters, 'Bring me $2,000 worth of ham and eggs.'"

Mitchell continued, "The next morning Matlock resplendent in a new loud suit of store clothing called from the street, 'Come down. I've got every blankety-wheeled vehicle in this blankety-blank place. Let's have some fun.' Forming a procession with Matlock in the lead, they made the rounds of town stopping at every saloon. Liquor flowed like a mountain torrent. The party lasted continuously for two days. Then Matlock departed for Portland and wider fields of joyous enterprises."

By 1903 Matlock was in the Eagle District, prospecting and mining on the Seventymile River, Nation River, 4th of July Creek and others. He spent his winters in Eagle, which was a lively community with Fort Egbert's soldiers still in the area. At one of the social functions he met Jessica Fox, a young English lady stranded in Eagle with her family. Jessica's father, Dr. Fox, an herb doctor, knew nothing about surviving in a northern environment. He had no skills with which to provide for his family. Jessica worked cleaning the school house for 75 cents an hour and Dr. Fox was working on the street. Matlock took the family out to 4th of July Creek with him and helped them get some mining claims.

Matlock and Jessica Fox were married after Thanksgiving, November 29, 1921. They went out to the creeks together where Jessica worked as a mining cook. The pair made quite a contrast. George was a rough, coarse type, considerably older than Jessica, while she was a minute cultured, fastidious person, whose English background was very evident not only in her speech and mannerism but also in her dress. She had lovely linens and china which she used daily, as she liked to cook and entertain. Though she divorced George later to marry Archie Mather, she always spoke kindly of him.

Matlock remained in the Eagle area with his partner Charlie Martin, continuing his prospecting and mining, trapping and hunting and working for others on their claims. In 1923 he was superintendent of operations for the Fourth of July Mining Company, during the time they hand dug a ten mile long ditch to carry water to their operations. Matlock and Charlie Martin built a cabin together on the Seventymile River. They often worked for Froelich and Kummer at Crooked Creek. Matlock was one of the six Seventymile miners who co-owned and shared a cabin in Eagle City which they all used intermittently.

One year while floating down the north fork of the Fortymile river near Moose Creek with his partner, their raft capsized. There was a large black-looking rock in the center of the creek which both men were able to climb up on. The rock looked interesting, so

GEORGE MATLOCK AND JESSICA FOX'S WEDDING PARTY 1921
Courtesy: Eagle Historical Socity

Matlock put a piece of it in his coat pocket. The men finally made
it to shore and built a fire to dry out. There were several old
stumps in the area as it was the regular crossing which the Indians
from Joseph Village had used. The trees had been felled using a
sharp rock for a wedge and hitting it with a club, like the Indians
used to do prior to the availability of iron. The men continued
floating down the river and swamped their raft again. This time
Matlock lost his coat which had the ore in the pocket.

Several years later, Matlock met a trader at Circle who used to
travel to Joseph's Village using the old river crossing. The
trader had also seen the unusual large black rock in the north
fork; in fact, he had sent a sample to the assayer and was told it
was gold telluride, a rich form of gold ore. George couldn't get
that rock out of his mind. It was fifteen years before he was able
to return to look for it. The creek and the country had changed and
he couldn't locate it, but he spent his last years looking for it.

In 1932, Matlock talked young Fred Terwilliger into going to the

Middle Fork with him to find that elusive black rock. Matlock
would furnish the grub. Fred cut the wood for Matlock's prospecting, cutting long trenches in many directions, using two fires each
day; he trapped on the side. Matlock was getting along in years
and had heart trouble. He would go out on snowshoes and get tired,
then rest a little around the camp, but he wouldn't give up. He
had trouble bending over, but he refused any help.

The second year in October 1933, they were packing in again over
the Champagne Creek trail and Matlock complained of being dizzy.
It had been a long day in the cold rain. They had lost their coats
off the pack horses and it bothered Matlock. Fred suggested they
could return to town, but George said, "No, might as well wear out
as to rust out."

During the first week they were at the Middle Fork cabin, Fred shot
a moose up on the mountainside. When he returned to the cabin for
his pack board, Matlock insisted upon putting on his pack board and
going with him. When Fred had almost reached the moose, he looked
back for Matlock. He had fallen down in the trail and by the time
Fred reached him, he was dead. Fred struggled to get Matlock back
to the cabin and covered with a blanket. He left him in the cabin
and went back to Eagle for help to bring in his body. There was a
lot of overflow on the creeks and it was November before they could
return with their dogs and sled. When they reached the body, a
weasel had eaten off half of Matlock's face. They brought his body
back to Eagle where he was buried.

John Powers was the administrator of Matlock's estate. George had
been drawing a pension from the Territory for several years. The
appraised value of all his property was $433.50. After his burial
expenses were paid, the residue from his estate was $26.24 which
was paid to the Treasurer of the Territory of Alaska on November
29, 1935.

ERWIN A. 'NIMROD' ROBERTSON
1855-1946

Nimrod was a cultured Scottish gentleman from Maine, who never lost
his Down East accent. He received the nickname of Nimrod when he
was a young man. As Captain of the National Guard of Bangor, he
had won the President's Match in marksmanship in the early 1890's.
In Maine he had been a hunter and guide.

The Robertsons came from the Scottish Highlands and were a very
large and interesting clan. They traced their ancestry to King
Malcolm in 1005. King Duncan of Macbeth fame is an ancestor. In
1768, Robert Robertson moved from Aberdeenshire, Scotland to
Saratoga, New York with his wife and four children. Robert fought
in the Revolutionary War, as did his eldest son, William. His wife
was a Tory and offered his services to the British, but that didn't
last long as Robert fled and joined the American cause. Nimrod's
father fought in the Civil War and was wounded twice.

For fifteen years Nimrod had practiced the trade of jeweler.
In the summer of 1898, with a group of five men from his home town,
Nimrod, now 43 years old, headed for Alaska over the Chilkoot Pass.
A variety of dreams brought these early gold miners to the
Klondike. Nimrod's dream was to build a flying machine. He
estimated he needed $1,000 to construct his 'bird machine' and
Eagle was as good a place as any to accumulate that amount. Nimrod
made his home in Eagle during the winter but spent his summers on
his gold claims on Flume Creek, a subsidiary of the Seventymile
River, searching for that elusive gold.

Nimrod spent more than 40 years at Flume Creek, but he was never a
successful miner, as he only worked when the spirit moved him. He
really didn't care much for mining. He preferred to fish, hunt and
trap for his own needs. His two dogs, pet mice and pet wolverine
kept him company. Many months he had nothing to eat except what he
could get off of the country. He had to eat his fish without salt
and he had no grease to fry them in, so they were always boiled.
He tried making flour out of the wild seeds. He was a gourmet chef
when he had the makings, which was not often.

Nimrod spent his winters in Eagle where he had a cabin and jewelry
shop. He enjoyed the city fellowship and attended all the social
functions which highlighted the village life. He went through all
the chairs at the Eagle Lodge of the Improved Order of Redmen. He
served on the Common Council of Eagle City intermittently from 1912
to 1940 as a member, chairman, Chief of Police, Marshal, Magistrate
and Attorney.

With such a busy life, Nimrod never found the time nor the money to
build his 'bird machine', though he never lost interest. Even
after hearing of the Wright Brothers first successful airplane
flight in Dec. 1903, he was not discouraged. In the 1930's when

ERWIN A. "NIMROD" ROBERTSON
Courtesy: Eagle Historical Society

after hearing of the Wright brothers first successful airplane
flight in Dec. 1903, he was not discouraged. In the 1930's when
Ernie Pyle traveled down the Yukon River gathering material for his
book Home Country, he stopped in Eagle and interviewed E. A.
Robertson. Nimrod told him, "If I had had a thousand dollars, I'd
have flown long before the other fellows, but I'm not much nearer
to my accomplishment than I was 40 years ago.".

They say necessity is the mother of invention. In Eagle Nimrod
found many necessities which called for his ingenuity and skill.
Though he was a jeweler by profession, he preferred to spend his
time working on inventions. They said that Nimrod could make
anything, except a living. He was a genius, always working on some
gadget to make his door open and close automatically, or tinkering
over his airplane model and other things that were never completed.
He made excellent snowshoes, was an artist with knitting needles
and could tan leather as soft as chamois to make his moccasins.
Time was nothing to Nimrod and he had the patience of Job. He

64

repaired watches and his handmade knives and gold puzzle rings made
him famous.

The hunting knives which Nimrod made were popular items. The
blades were ground down from large wood files and tempered by a
secret process. Even his closest friends never learned how he
created the nail cutting blade. He used to demonstrate the cutting
edge by trimming the corrugation off a silver dollar as easily as
you could peel an orange with a paring knife.

Nimrod's dental reputation spread as far as Seattle, as the man who
shot a bear, made himself a pair of dentures from the bear's teeth
with which he ate the bear. In 1905 Nimrod had scurvy and lost all
of his teeth. He decided to make himself a pair of false teeth.
He used spruce pitch to make the impressions, sheep teeth for the
four front teeth, caribou teeth back of those and bear teeth for
the molars. He set the teeth in aluminum, melted down from an old
pot in his cabin.

Clare Burke wrote that Nimrod was a frequent guest for Sunday night
suppers at the Fort Yukon Mission House (Burke, 1961). "Nimrod had
the distinction of possessing the only known set of dentures made
from bear's teeth, set by affixing the teeth in plates he had
forged from an aluminum pot lid. They served him well except that
the metal heated uncomfortably when he drank hot tea or coffee. He
overcame this difficulty by removing his bear's teeth when he drank
hot liquids." They couldn't blame him, but it was a little dis-
concerting to see bear teeth with aluminum gums grinning at them
from the table. Nimrod later went to Seattle to get himself a set
of nonheating teeth. He found a dentist who made an even exchange
as he was intrigued by the bear teeth plates. But the new teeth
were uncomfortable and did not chew as well as his old ones and he
wished he had his old bear's teeth back. Nimrod served as the
dentist for his neighbors as no one was better trained to do the
work. He pulled teeth and filled them to suit the taste of each
individual.
At the request of the Common Council of Eagle, Nimrod made a 60" x
80" relief map of the Eagle area in 1909. It was made out of
newspapers and magazines digested into pulp and colored with
Hematite iron ore and moose blood. It was made from his intimate
knowledge of the countryside by hiking all through the Eagle back
country. The map was sent to Seattle twice for display; first in
1905 to the Alaska-Yukon-Pacific Exposition and again in 1962 to
the World's Fair in Seattle.

Present day residents of Eagle have many memories associated with
Nimrod, including his fondness for children. He was soft spoken and
gentle and never swore. When he drove his dog team, he would say,
"Get along there now or I shall damn you." Others remember him as
a religious recluse, praying about everything and often preaching
a sermon to himself each Sunday.

Nimrod lived out his long life in Eagle. He had only made the one
trip outside to Seattle during his 40 year Alaska residency and he
had no plans to return. In the fall of 1940, he decided to make a
prospecting trip to the mouth of the Seventymile to look at some
placer ground he had staked that summer. He only intended to stay
a few days. Suddenly it turned cold in early November. The ice
was running too heavy to return by the river. His provisions were
exhausted. He started across country to Eagle, twenty miles by an
old trail which had not been used since 1900. He was half way home
when he became so weak and tired, he could go no farther. He was
numb with cold but could not get a fire started. Nimrod realized
his time had come. He stood his rifle against a tree, hung his
field glasses on a bush, laid down in a creek bed and pulled his
parka hood over his face, folded his arms and dropped off to sleep,
never to awaken. It was a peaceful end for he had not stirred from
that position.

The Eagle residents became worried over Nimrod's late return home.
A search party was organized but it took them many days to find him
on the unused trail. They learned from his diary they found in his
pack, that he had laid there twelve days. His body was frozen
solid. A warm spell had come and the glacier water filled in the
depression where he lay and in another few days all would have been
out of sight in the ice. It took some time to chop him out of the
ice and later to thaw out his body to get it in a coffin. The
Improved Order of Redmen held his funeral November 29, 1940 and
Nimrod was laid to rest in the Eagle Cemetery.

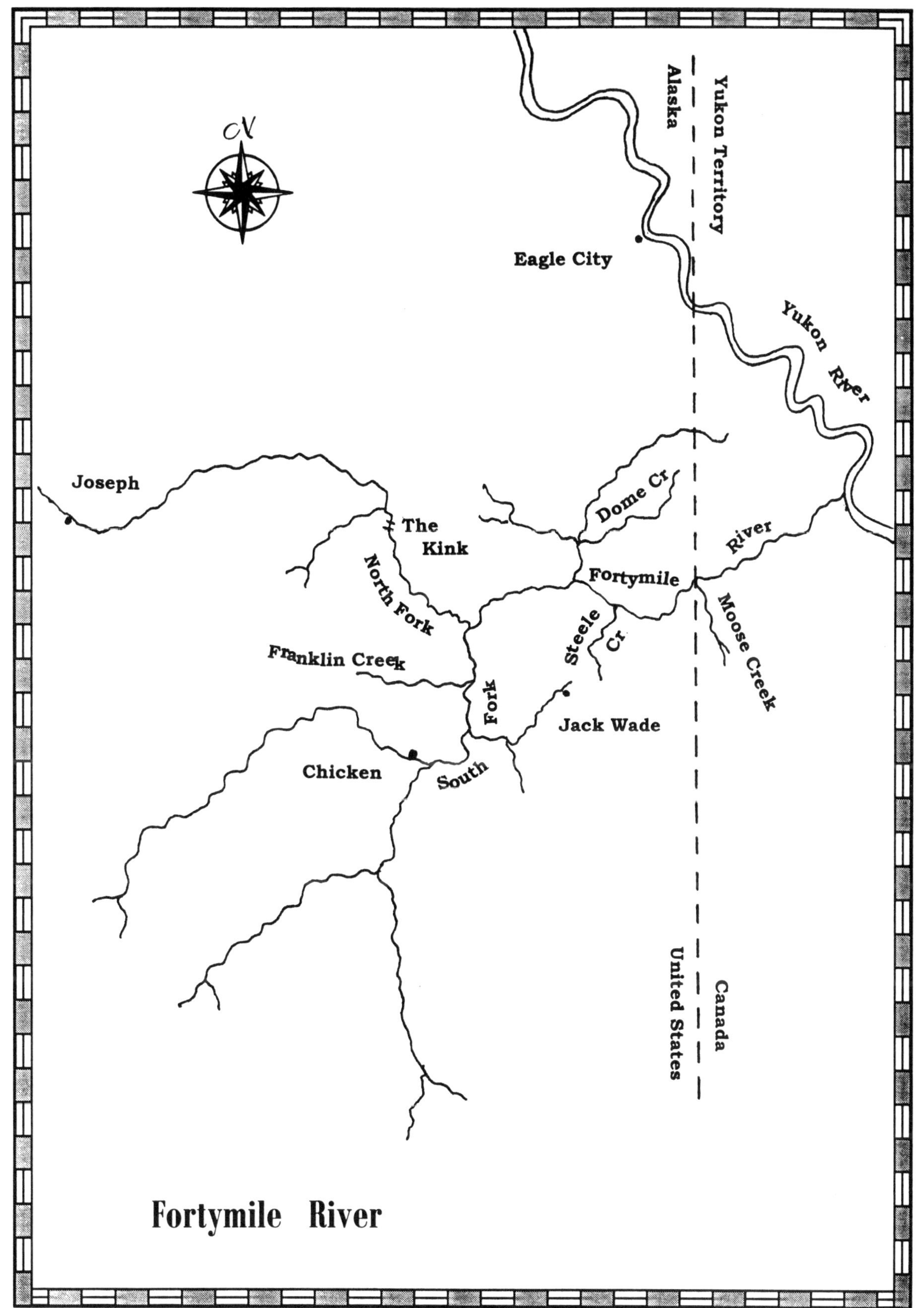

Alaska
Yukon Territory
Yukon River
Eagle City
Joseph
The Kink
North Fork
Dome Cr
Fortymile
River
Franklin Creek
Steele Cr
Moose Creek
South Fork
Jack Wade
Chicken
South Fork
United States
Canada
Fortymile River

PETERSEN BROTHERS

THE KINK

One interesting mining story concerns "The Kink", a two mile stretch of the south-fork of the Fortymile River that twists back on to itself, with a steep hill separating the two sides of the horseshoe bend, thus receiving its appropriate name.

News of the Klondike gold rush reached Horne, Denmark and two brothers, Johannes and Emile Petersen, caught the gold fever and decided to seek their fortune. Johannes, the youngest, celebrated his 16th birthday on their trek over the Chilkoot Trail on March 29, 1898. They came prepared with enough provisions to last them eighteen months, so they had several tons to pack over the mountain, but they were a hardy pair. They each crossed 30 to 40 times with 50 pound packs on their backs each trip. They joined up with other hikers forming a group of nine in their party, built a boat and traveled together down river to Dawson where they arrived on June 24th with seventeen tons of supplies.

Finding no open mining claims worth prospecting in the Klondike, they proceeded to the Fortymile River. On July 6th they traveled 95 miles up the river from the City of Fortymile. There they found some promising color in their pans and in 1898 they recorded nine claims on a portion of the river that was locally known as the Kink.

Emile went outside to file the claims, organize a company, raise money and work in a machine shop in Chicago where he built some of the equipment they needed for their mining. They recorded the claims with the gold commissioner in Sitka, under the name Northfork Bedrock Mining Co., Northfork, Fortymile river. After forming the company, they sent for their brothers Earl and Hans Christian. The financier of the operation was Mr. Harry Bauer, son of an English Lord, living in Chicago. Johannes stayed alone all winter to hold the claims, with only a horse and dog for company.

The next summer all four brothers worked on the river bars. The work was going too slowly to suit them, as they had bigger dreams. They thought there was a lot of gold in the river bed, which they could not mine due to the depth of the water. With the kink in the river, why not change the course of the river so they would have a dry river bed to mine? They decided to try it.

Two of the brothers spent the winter of 1899 outside. Whey they returned they brought in 600# of dynamite, a sawmill, steam driller and an 8 horse-power steam engine which they put in a 10'x 40' boat to carry their twelve tons of provisions. By this time a railroad had been built from Skagway to Lake Bennett which carried their supplies. On June 19, 1900 they traveled down the Yukon by steam to Dawson, but their new boat didn't work so well going up stream on

DYNAMITING MOUNTAIN ON FORTYMILE RIVER
Courtesy: Yukon Archives, Whitehorse

the swift Fortymile River. It took them 22 days to winch the boat up to the American border (23 miles). There they left half of their provisions and built a smaller boat which they steamed up to Steele Creek. The rest of the goods were brought up by sledge over the ice in the winter.

The men set to work immediately on their project. They had hired three experienced men to dynamite the cut through the mountain to change the course of the river. They worked for four weeks, agreeing to pay each man $5 a day if they found good gold; if no good gold, no payment. It cost the Danes $3 to $4 a day to feed each man, even though they used a lot of fish and a caribou.

On October 3rd, the fourteen foot cut was completed and the river gushed through its new channel. They couldn't wait to find what they had in that two miles of solid rock river bed. They examined

FORTYMILE RIVER CHANGED COURSE
Courtesy: Yukon Archives, Whitehorse

an area 100' x 125' and determined it would pay about fifteen cents
a foot or about $20,000 and some bars looked better. Working their
dry river bed by hand proved to be inefficient; they needed some
modern equipment. With their sluice boxes, they took out enough
gold along one side of the river bed to pay for another trip
outside. Emile was again selected to travel out during the winter
of 1900 to get more money for equipment while the others remained
to protect the claims. The rest of the men continued prospecting
all winter.

Emile obtained the finances and returned with eight horses and
large horse drawn fresnos. With those they could take large scoops
of pay dirt to the sluice boxes with their horses. Mr. Bauer, their
financier, visited them during the summer bringing a Kodak camera,
he recorded the whole operation. In 1901 the hole in the mountain
filled in with a rock slide. The Petersen party returned to Denmark.

MINING DRY RIVER BED
Courtesy: Yukon Archives, Whitehorse

This interesting story became known today when Johannes Petersen's son traveled to Eagle with his family in 1988 to see "The Kink" where his father had mined. Luckily there was a helicopter in the area, from which they could view the former mining grounds. Before leaving, they were asked how the Petersen party had done financially. He responded, "They never earned big money, but neither did they have a loss."

On May 26, 1913, William Wehner of Evergreen, California filed a complaint with the Attorney General of the U. S. charging that in 1900 Alexander Bauer of Chicago caused the navigation of the north-fork of the Fortymile River to be utterly destroyed by creating a waterfall, where before the waters were slowly winding their way to the main river. The north-fork's normal width was 300' and before the change was navigable for large rafts and boats. In its present condition it could not be navigated at this point as the fall is

ROCK SLIDE CLOSES MOUNTAIN CUT
Courtesy: Yukon Archives, Whitehorse

twenty-three feet and below a turn in the river, making it exceedingly dangerous and in all probability lives have been lost there. The complaint requested an investigation.

The complaint was answered by a letter from the Deputy Commissioner at Eagle to Major Cavanaugh, Corps of Engineers, Seattle, WA on August 11, 1913 and contained the following information. The obstruction mentioned by Mr. Wehner occurred at what is known locally as the 'Big Kink.' For the purpose of laying bare and placer mining the stream bed around the bend, Mr. Bauer diverted the stream across the neck of land where it has flowed ever since. Prior to the diversion, the stream was of doubtful capacity for floating log rafts. Only small row boats could or can ascend it and these have to be drawn by hand line or polled. The diversion by Bauer did not interfere with small boating in the summer or sledding supplies over the frozen surface in winter.

CHAPTER 6

EDUCATION

Following the purchase of Alaska from Russia in 1867, education
passed through what is known as a 'dark age'. Russian schools were
closed in the major communities and the government did little to
replace them, though some American church denominations opened a
few mission schools, helping to fill the void. Finally in 1884, an
Act was approved which provided for education in Alaska under the
direction of the Department of the Interior, Bureau of Education,
but neither the church schools nor the government schools reached
into the interior as far as the Eagle area.

By the time large numbers of miners started congregating around
Eagle, the indigenous Indians were already settled into a village,
but no formal education was offered. The 1900 Civil Code not only
provided for City incorporation, but also the organization of a
City school district. The school was financed with 50% of the
receipts from the local business licenses and taxes. The first
school in Eagle was opened September 1901 in a rented log cabin
with seven students. Mrs. Sarah McComb, the teacher, was paid $100
a month.

NEW EAGLE CITY SCHOOL 1903
Courtesy: Cameron Collection, EHS

The log cabin school was outgrown in two years, and a new building on the school reserve property was completed June 25, 1903. The students had a new teacher that year, Miss Lois Adams. The first school term was from July 1 to November 20 and the second term started February 19 so the students were home during the dark, cold months of winter.

The City School continued until 1955 with the teachers remaining an average of two years. The school was closed intermittently during that time, due to a lack of students. During the closures city students attended schools in Dawson, Eagle Village, visited relatives or missed a year.

Eagle Village was located three miles up river from Eagle City but did not have a school. The Indians did not mix freely in the white community, though they came into town to work, trade at the stores or receive medical care, but did not attend the incorporated school in Eagle City. When the Presbyterian missionaries, Rev. & Mrs. Ensign, arrived in Eagle in 1902, Mrs. Ensign opened a day school for the Indian children with fourteen enrolled. The children walked the three miles each way to Eagle City.

After 1905, the Episcopal Church personnel offered a day school in the Village chapel for all ages of Indians. Music was especially enjoyed. George Boulter was appointed teacher and Lay Reader, his average school attendance was 25. The Episcopal Church deeded the lot next to the church in the village for a school site. A new log structure was completed in October 1900 which contained a single classroom and a teacher's residence. The Bureau of Indian Affairs began to provide the village teachers. In 1909, there were 34 students enrolled between the ages of 4 and 60. Though one teacher remained in the village for 13 years, the average length of residence for the other teachers was two years.

The teacher was a key figure in the village. Not only were they charged with the educational responsibilities, but were also called upon to serve as the social worker, lawyer, doctor, midwife, gardener, counselor and anything else that needed to be done.

When the village school closed in 1945 due to lack of students, the city school resumed operations. A few of the native students attended the city school, but some had missed nine years of education. In 1955, the tables were reversed; when the city school closed for the last time due to lack of students, the Bureau of Indian Affairs reopened the village school. The original log school building had been through a major flood and was looking its age. In 1963, the BIA built a large new school which included one classroom, teacher's quarters, medical clinic, office, storage rooms and school kitchen. The facility was located in the village but was open to all the children in the area.

In 1967, the State of Alaska assumed the responsibility for the

Eagle Village school for both the City and Village students. In
1969, there were 10 Indian students and 11 white students attending
and it was necessary to start operating a school bus.

Until 1975, the Eagle school held classes for grades one through
eighth. For high school the students had the choice of attending
regional high schools or continuing their education at home with a
correspondence program. In 1975 there were six correspondence high
school students who met afternoons in the old city school for
supervised study. The next year, in an effort to meet the require-
ments of the Hootch Consent settlement (which required high schools
in villages with eight or more high school age students), high
school was held in the newly restored Wickersham Courthouse, but it
was found to be unsuitable. The large BIA Village school was then
remodeled to include three classrooms, plus a relocatable classroom
and the teaching staff was increased to four.

The Village facilities were more than adequate for the 40 students,
but the State of Alaska's cup runneth over with oil money. A large
multi-million dollar school building was built in Eagle City in
1985 for grades K-12.

EAGLE PUBLIC LIBRARY

Books, magazines and any printed word were very important to the
citizens of Eagle. Reading rooms were quickly established at the
church, the fort, the lodges and business houses. In 1901, Judge
Wickersham was instrumental in establishing a public library in
Eagle.

In 1938 Jessica Mather started the present incorporated Eagle
Public Library in the Courthouse. Funds were raised with their card
games. It soon outgrew it's space and in 1976, a 34'x50' log
building was constructed. The library, with all their books,
magazines, videos, computers, etc., continues to be popular with
both the city and the village residents.

EAGLE HISTORICAL SOCIETY

When the Taylor Highway into Eagle was completed in 1953, the
residents began to realize the importance of all the old abandoned,
deteriorating cabins and government buildings in Eagle. To preserve
their history, the Eagle Historical Society was organized and
incorporated in 1961. Since that date, they have been instrumental
in the restoration of seven of the large historic buildings and in
the collection of local artifacts which is exhibited in five of the
restored museum buildings. Tours are given daily during the summer
months. The museums, with their exhibits, buildings, archives and
photograph collection, have become the major source of the history
of the Eagle area and provide a rich educational experience to both
the local community and the visitors.

Borghilde Henriksen was born in Lyngor, Norway in 1897. At the age of two, she traveled to the United States with her recently widowed mother and was raised in North Dakota with one half-sister and two half-brothers.

She attended the Chicago Training School, where she studied to be a teacher and missionary. While attending the institute in 1924, she met Lydia, a nurse who had worked several years for the Bureau of Indian Affairs (BIA) in Alaska. Borghilde developed an interest in Alaska and applied to the BIA as a teacher or any other position she might be able to fill. In August 1925, she received a telegram from the BIA office in Seattle. It read, "Opening for grade school teacher, Eagle, Alaska. If interested proceed to Seattle as soon as possible." Preparations began by investing in a minimum amount of warm clothing and an eider down comforter.

Within a week she was aboard a Seattle bound train and soon on a ship sailing out of Puget Sound. Borghilde experienced a dreadful feeling of loneliness mingled with uncertainty as she boarded the ship. She really knew very little of what lay ahead, but she was on her way.

Her voyage ended at Skagway where she boarded the White Pass and Yukon train to Whitehorse, and then a river steamer for her journey down the Yukon River. Arriving in Dawson, Borghilde learned she would have to wait nine days to go to Eagle with Percy DeWolfe in his mail launch. They made the 100 mile trip in good time. Percy introduced her to several of the town's people and to the manager of the Riverside Hotel who had been holding a room for her for two weeks.

In the morning she questioned the ways and means of getting the three miles to the Indian Village which was her real destination. She learned she might get a horse but the safest way was to walk. It was a beautiful day and the scenery was gorgeous so she decided to walk. After walking a mile or so, Borghilde heard voices in a foreign tongue. She stopped to listen and there before her stood two young men, both definitely Indian and both very friendly. They introduced themselves and she learned the village people had been looking for her for a long time. Nearing the village she could see people all along the bank waiting to get their first glimpse of the new teacher.

Esau was the Village Chief and he introduced her to his people. Having the key to the school and her quarters, he showed her the facilities. Telling Esau she needed to get her luggage and food to the village, he promised that a couple of the boys would bring them up in a poling boat.

The only boats they had were poling boats and the small one man canoes. There were still a few birch bark canoes but most of them were the wood/canvas type which were easier to make and repair. Often these people used their dogs to pull their boats upstream, fastening a line from the boat to the team. This worked fine especially with a well-trained leader.

The teacher's supplies arrived the next day. It didn't take long to get settled and to open school. There were 25 students; several were beginners. With two to four in each of the nine grades, it took a while to arrange classes. They didn't understand her language and she didn't understand theirs. They all agreed to help one another and Borghilde fell in love with the children at once. She soon found that teaching was only a fraction of her duties. She had to pretend to be doctor, nurse and midwife. That was difficult. One of her early patients was a middle aged lady in the last stages of tuberculosis.

About the middle of November, a man came to the school and said his wife was having a baby and she needed to come. Borghilde asked if he had called Sarah Walters who had helped with so many deliveries. He said, "No, we don't need her," to which Borghilde replied, "Yes we do." So he grunted and left. Sarah was there and soon there was also a new husky boy. A second baby was born in February, and after that so many arrived Borghilde lost count.

There was little chance of going to a hospital and doctor for delivery although there were hospitals at both Dawson and Fort Yukon. The steamboat made three trips a month during the summer months, but what mother could afford to spend a month or more away from home just to have a baby? In the winter time, there wasn't even a chance to get there. So babies, illnesses or accidents, you stayed at home and did the best you could.

Borghilde had quite an experience during the river break-up in the spring of 1937. The entire village was flooded and had to be evacuated. The Chief moved everyone up on the hillside at 4 a.m., taking tents, bedding and food. While they were spending their second day on the hill behind the village, Borghilde suggested that someone should furnish another tent, so she could teach classes. A tent was located and two men took her to the school in a boat for supplies. There was still six feet of water in some of the cabins and two feet in the school. The men took the boat to the back window, through which Borghilde stepped into the cold water. She hurriedly gathered a few things, having to step carefully as the cellar door in the middle of the floor was open. The cellar, full of water, had pushed the door open. After three armloads to the boat, the men told her she had enough, to get back in the boat. She did, as she was chilled by that time. They had school in the tents for three weeks with the older children attending in the morning and the little ones in the afternoon. The children seemed to enjoy it as it was so different.

BORGHILDE "OLE" HENRIKSEN 1932
Courtesy: Eagle Historical Society

The flood didn't take out any of the houses, but it took everything
else. Lumber, wood and dog houses all floated away. It took quite
awhile for the village to dry out enough so they could move back.

Borghilde taught school in Eagle Village for thirteen years, until
the spring of 1938. After marrying an Eagle miner, Burnett F.
Hansen in July 1938, they moved to Fairbanks. A son, Jim, was born
November 12, 1939. The family returned to the Eagle area in 1944,
to spend summers on the creeks mining for gold. They returned to
Eagle for the winter. In 1948, Borghilde substituted one semester
in the Eagle City School.

Between 1951 and 1955, Borghilde served as the city postmaster,
weatherman and custom's agent. These jobs required her to stay in
Eagle year round. Because she missed being out at the mining camp
with her family in the summers, she resigned.

Borghilde always maintained a special interest in the Indians at
Eagle Village. They visited her regularly in town; they kept her in

78

touch with all of the village activities. When there were problems
in the village, she would quietly say, "Oh, how I wish I could have
taught them more."

1961 was the last year the Hansens mined. They continued living in
Eagle in spite of both Barney's and Ole's poor health. After
Barney's death in 1977, Borghilde resided full time at the
Fairbanks Pioneer Home until her death in December, 1983. Her body
was laid to rest in the Eagle cemetery, beside her beloved husband,
58 years after the quiet young lady had arrived in this new and
strange land.

                            ILOE SLADE O'NEILL
                    Eagle City School teacher 1927-1928

After two and one half years of University and normal school work,
and three years of teaching in southeast Alaska and Chitina, Iloe
Slade headed for Eagle in September 1927. Reading about the Yukon
River and the north-central part of Alaska and seeing it on the map
did little to prepare her for traveling on that river. See found
the rapids and rapid flow of the river to be exciting. The scenery,
the tree and shrub growth on the banks of the river were different
than any she had seen anywhere else in Alaska. It had only taken 6
1/2 hours for the sternwheeler to make the 100 mile trip from
Dawson.

Mr. Charles Ott, Chairman of the School Board, met the boat and
escorted Miss Slade to the Riverside Hotel where she lived for the
school year. The hotel was very much like a road house. It was
comfortable and efficiently run by Mr. and Mrs. Randall. Their son,
Cyril, was in the 8th grade. Her room faced the river with a lovely
view. Iloe watched fascinated as the ice started flowing down the
river. About this time, there was ice in her water pitcher in the
mornings. Washing in ice water was a new experience. After a few
discussions with Mrs. Randall and an O.K. from Percy DeWolfe, the
mail carrier from Dawson, for whom the room across the hall was
reserved for his twice a month mail trips, Iloe moved across the
hall to a room with a brick chimney going through it. It was
comfortably warm all winter and while she still washed in cold
water, it never again had ice on it.

Mrs. Randall served excellent meals and several retired bachelors
always had their dinners there. Caribou was the usual meat and
occasionally moose meat with sheep being the best. They had a sheep
roast for their Christmas dinner served with local cranberries,
mashed home grown potatoes, gravy and homemade bread--a grand meal.

The school was a one room building of frame construction with an
attached shed for wood storage and out houses. The wood stove in
the center of the room, was a problem at first as the fire had to
be started every morning and it took some time to heat the room
even after the children arrived. As the temperature dropped, the
problem increase. Without too much persuasion, the school board
hired a man living close by to stoke the fire at night and get it
going in the morning. One gas lamp provided the light.

The children were in five grades with no more than one or two in
each grade. This made for a very busy full day without time for
anything but the basics. Fortunately the children were all well
behaved so they had no social problems. There was a lot of make up
work to be done. The teacher was concerned about grade progress,
but was pleased with most of the work accomplished.

Iloe wrote that the winter seemed long, especially when it was dark

going to school and dark returning home. The sun was a welcome
sight after an absence of six weeks even if only a fragment of it
appeared above the horizon at first. Each day a slight increase was
noted until the full sun shone. Everyone rejoiced to have the
longer daylight and warmer temperatures. During the winter the
sixty below temperature was sometimes accompanied by a strong wind
which would redeposit the snow in unusual places and high drifts.

The favorite winter pastime was playing bridge. Mr. Ott, Dover, Ted
Ofstead and Iloe had a continuous game going all winter right after
dinner. Mr. Ott and Mr. Dover had their dinners at the hotel so it
was convenient for all of them. The score was kept for the entire
winter and was a long one. Iloe also enjoyed dinner and bridge at
the Turnbulls. Mrs. Turnbull was a congenial lady with whom Iloe
did her first snowshoeing. She also went horseback riding with Mrs.
Turnbull after the snow was gone.

The Vicar of the Anglican Church and his wife used to have Iloe for
tea on Wednesdays after which snow, that the children had
collected, was melted and heated, in order to bathe. That was a
real treat. After their son, John, was born, they no longer had the
time to indulge Iloe in that luxury.

The Red Men's supper dance was the social event of the year. The
baked ham and trimmings were unusually good and the dancing, music
by phonograph records--fox trots and waltzes only--was great.
Everyone participated and because there were so few women, they all
danced every dance and were weary people by the evenings end.

The three mile trip by foot or dogteam to the Native Village was
always interesting. Borghilde Henrikson, who was teaching there,
was most hospitable and friendly. She had taken in two of the local
children whose mother was ill and later died. She was a true mother
to them. It was through her that Iloe got to observe how the native
men of the village organized a Potlatch. It started with a small
group of men with a blanket knocking at every door in the village.
When the door was opened, out came a can of tomatoes or other
vegetables, canned fruit, frozen meat or berries or whatever to be
tossed into the blanket. This was then taken to their social hall
where the meat and vegetables were cooked into an excellent stew.
The stew was then served on white enameled plates with the women
and children sitting at one table and the men at another. When
finished, each woman loaded her plate with whatever was left--
canned peaches, frozen berries and anything else--and took it to
their homes. It was this same evening that Iloe danced her first
Red River jig. The Chief of the tribe stood in front of her
indicating she was to dance with him. This consisted of sort of
hopping on one foot and of scratching with the other as you circled
with your partner until someone comes to relieve you. In this case
it was Borghilde. Iloe always enjoyed her visits to the village.

During the winter, Mrs. Robinson, the only black woman in Eagle, died. Iloe went to see her shortly before, when Mrs. Robinson had told her that she was to tired to talk. She lived in a small cabin and did laundry for some of the town's people. A collection was taken for her burial and Iloe was surprised the next year to have the amount of her donation returned by the executor of the estate.

Besides Iloe's work at school, another rewarding experience was teaching the local Marshal's wife, to read and write. She was an Indian lady from Tanana and was an able learner. Within a short time she was able to sign for a package at the postoffice with a great deal of pride. She made Iloe two pairs of beautifully beaded moosehide moccasins. One pair was for dancing with a strap around the ankle.

The spring breakup of the ice in the river was a big event to all the town's people. When the ice broke or melted from the banks, they had fresh grayling. They were a real treat from the winter's diet of large game. The breakup presaged the warm weather, beautiful days and activities that would follow.

The school board asked Iloe to return for the next school year, but Iloe had already accepted a teaching position at the school at Kennicott. She left with warm feelings for Eagle and it's people on the first boat down river that spring.

ANNE HOBBS PURDY
1901-1987

Anne Hobbs was born November 10, 1901 in the worst part of the back country of Missouri. She spent most of her early childhood with her maternal grandmother, who was illiterate and part Cherokee, on her rundown farm in Missouri. Her parents migrated to the coal fields in Colorado where her father was an engineer, taking care of the machinery. They lived all over Colorado. When grown, Anne went to Oregon as a teacher in 1924 and to Alaska in 1927.

It was late in the summer of 1927 when she arrived in Eagle on a sternwheeler. As her teaching assignment was in Chicken, she had to take a pack train from Eagle City to reach her destination eighty miles away. Enroute, it alternately rained, snowed, hailed, and the sun beat down; the mosquitos were out in full force. Every place they stopped, a man would give her something to wear. First a pair of Stanfield underwear from a real tall donor. Then a pair of bib overalls and rubber boats, the swamp wear type. Anne said once she got off the horse, she could hardly get back on with all the heavy clothing. When they rode into the little town of Chicken, they stopped at the post office, but she couldn't get off the horse. An old timer said he would help her off and he got a potato crate which he put by the horse to use for a step. The box was not a strong one and down she went in the mud. Nobody laughed, but that was the way she arrived in Chicken. She was soon settled in her one room cabin.

There were freighters on the Fortymile River with horses and they often stayed with Anne. The stables were right across from the school house. When she knew they were coming, she would start a fire in the barn for the horses and the freighters would go over and eat with her. They were surprised that she could cook. They got along fine until the weather turned real cold. The freighters brought over all their perishables for her to keep. Anne didn't know what perishables were. She only had the one room and Alice Roberts, a student, was staying with her, so they were crowded. She put everything on the floor where the perishables promptly froze solid, thus ending her friendship with the freighters.

Life was different those years. If you wanted to go anywhere you just walked. They had dances and parties, usually a dance every two weeks at the school house which everybody attended. Everyone had wild meat, wild berries and good gardens which they shared.

Thirty miles up the Fortymile River from Chicken there was an old village called Ketchumstock. There were still a few Indians living there when Anne first arrived. Tuberculosis was very prevalent at that time, from which most of the Indians had died. The remaining Indians used to go down to Chicken to trade. While teaching at Chicken and Franklin, Anne adopted a three year old half Indian girl.

Anne taught school in Chicken from September until January. Then she would go to Franklin to teach for five months. They went down the Fortymile river to Franklin in a hay wagon when it was 65 degrees below zero and Anne nearly froze. When they reached Robert's Roadhouse at Franklin, she said she had never been so cold in all her life. She finally went to sleep, but she was cold all night. When she woke up in the morning, she kept yanking on the covers, but they had frozen solid to the wall.

Anne taught at Franklin three consecutive seasons. The school was built with green logs. It was one room which served as both living quarters and school room. Isabel Purdy, from Chicken, was staying with her. Anne had five pupils and felt she had done some of the best teaching of her life. The floor was so cold, they couldn't stand it. She had a three-quarter sized bed, so she put the kids up on the bed while she sat in the middle of it. Anne especially enjoyed watching the caribou come right by the school house. There was a little porch overlooking the Fortymile River. They could lie on the porch and reach out and touch the caribou. Thousands of them passed six deep, calves, cows and the big bulls. Everyone was so hungry for meat they killed a lot of caribou. Then they all ate so much fresh meat, it made them sick.

Franklin Creek, located about ten miles from Chicken, was the site of the big gold discovery in 1886. There were mostly men living in that area and if they didn't make $1.00 a day, they refused to work. A pretty good road from Dawson came into the country at Jack Wade Creek which was about 15 miles from Chicken. If you had a tooth ache or anything, you walked to Dawson, a distance of 100 miles. They used to go to Dawson a lot, walking over there just to shop.

Anne Hobbs moved to Eagle in 1930 where she taught at the Eagle City School for two years. There she met and married a miner, Barney Hansen. Barney and Anne did not have any children, but Anne had adopted four school age children, Jack, George, Ethel and Eddie. The Hansens soon separated and Anne returned to Chicken with her children. Later Anne Hansen returned to Eagle to teach three more years between 1936 and 1939. The Eagle School Board had been looking for a teacher with children to meet the required attendance level for the state to provide a teacher.

In 1940 she married Fred Purdy, a gold miner from Chicken. Anne said he was a fine man, part native, and they had a good marriage. They raised eleven adopted children. By 1975, Fred and three of the children had died.

Anne Purdy taught at the Eagle City School an additional year, 1945-46. Later she taught were at Hope, Dot Lake, Fairbanks, Tetlin Indian Village, plus in her home at Chicken for ten years. She started a school lunch program in Tetlin where she made homemade breads and soups for the children. With her ready smile and a twinkle in her bright blue eyes, Anne loved to tell the stories

ANNE & FRED PURDY'S WEDDING DAY IN EAGLE, 1940
Courtesy: Eagle Historical Society

of her many adventures.

Anne wrote a novel entitled <u>Dark Boundary</u> with Eagle as the setting
for the story. She was a freelance journalist and story writer, who
for many years wrote a column called 'Chicken Pickins' for the

Fairbanks Daily News-Miner. She also wrote stories for the Alaska Sportsman, the Guidepost Magazine and other publications. She worked on her autobiography for a number of years. Later this story was used as a basis for the novel _Tisha_, written by Robert Sprecht. The book became a best seller, was printed in five languages and brought Anne much notoriety plus many invitations to travel, all of which she enjoyed immensely. "Tisha" was a nickname given to her by the Tetlin school children, who could not pronounce "teacher".

In her last years, Anne spent summers in her Chicken home with her daughter, Lynn, hosting and entertaining many visitors who had traveled long distances to find her on the creek. She kept waiting in vain for the promised film crew which was supposed to arrive in Chicken to film parts of the novel _Tisha_. Winters were spent outside in the desert areas, visiting, traveling and working on a sequel to _Tisha_.

Anne died April 15, 1987 at the age of 85 in the home of a long time friend at Dot Lake. She had suffered a broken hip and a mild stroke the previous fall.

Jessica Mather lived a quiet life in Eagle in the big house on the waterfront after the death of her husband, Archie, in the late 1930's. She had a nice garden and gathered wood. She especially enjoyed entertaining her friends w:.th her special raspberry tarts with almond paste and serving tea on her fine china, all made most enjoyable with her spicy conversat:.on and sense of humor. She was an intelligent woman, well read and fun, frequently quoting from Dicken's Pickwick papers and other classics. Her well remembered quotes include 'running away with the ragged ends of truth,' and 'everyone is a little queer except thee and me.'

Jessica was a small lady, 5'2", thin in her early days, but developed a full hour glass figure in later years. She was a very tidy person, who always had a clean house with every thing in place. Her English background was always evident not only in her speech and mannerism but also in her dress. She wore old fashioned clothes and long hair put up in the back with tight curls which she curled on wooden sticks.

JESSICA FOX WITH HER FATHER, DR. FOX
Courtesy: Eagle Historical Society

Jessica liked to cook and entertain. She had lovely linen and china which she used daily. She frequently had dinner guests (dinner always included Sauterne wine) after which they played bridge or pinochle. Dances were held weekly and for special occasions, Jessica wore a long green velvet dress which added much splendor to the occasion. Socials were held after church services. They would all move into the rectory house where they would have coffee and cake, discussion and arguments and listen to music. Thursday night song gatherings were held at the church, with refreshments and cards following. Pinochle was a favorite winter pastime.

In 1908, Jessica made her first trip to America to visit her brother in California, returning six months later by way of New Orleans traveling from there to New York by 'that funny little sternwheeler, the Creole, and by the Lusitania across the Atlantic to England. In 1914, Jessica Fox traveled to North America with her parents, Dr. and Mrs. Fox. They came from Handsworth (near Sheffield), Yorkshire, England , which was reduced to rubble during World War II. They had lived in a house built in 1553. Jessica studied for the Cambridge degree in Sheffield. The family arrived in Dawson the 22nd of June, 1914 to visit her brother while he was working for Guggenheimer and Kennicott Copper. They had arrived in Eagle quite by accident. They had only planned a one year trip, but Jessica's mother became very ill and they had to leave the boat at the very first port over the American line. Before her mother was well enough to return to England, World War I had broken out. They had to stay in Eagle, because they wouldn't allow her mother to cross the ocean at that time.

The trunks which the Fox family had brought with them for their one year visit included china, a china closet, silver, linens, a French crystal clock, books and bookcases Although the Fox family lived with these luxury items, cash was in short supply as all of her father's money was tied up in England. Jessica said, "My father was a doctor and like all professional men, he wasn't very practical and I didn't know anything either. We had no commercial education. But by catching salmon and different things we did, we managed until the war was over." An early photograph shows Jessica in a nurses uniform as she used to assist her father who was a doctor of herbology.

Dr. Fox became interested in gold mining and worked out on Fox Creek with George Matlock, whom Jessica later married. Her earlier marriage in Dawson had been annulled. Though they were divorced later, Jessica always spoke kindly of him. The Fox family went out to the creek to mine for gold where Jessica worked as a camp cook.

Next the family went to 4th of July Creek, a tributary of the Seventymile River, where Jessica met Archie Mather, whom she married in 1925. He was a gentleman from New England who always called her 'lover.' After their marriage they mined in the Seventymile River area. Jessica and Archie moved to Fairbanks after

Archie injured his leg in a fall off a roof, which resulted in being hospitalized several months. The Mathers then returned to New England for his convalescence and planned to remain there, but 'mining was in his blood' and they returned to Alaska in the early 1930's. In March of 1939, after a long illness, Mr. Mather died of cancer of the brain at the Fairbanks Hospital and Jessica returned to Eagle.

Jessica loved good literature. She owned many well read leather bound classics which she cherished like old friends. Thus it only seems natural that she became the key person in reorganizing the Eagle Public Library in 1938, and retained an interest in it the rest of her life.

During the war years, 1941-45, Jessica returned to Fairbanks. She worked as a clerk in Charley Main's general store and did house work for Dr. Duckering at the University until she found work in the laundry. After the war, she returned to Eagle where she took up gardening, and cooking for a living, supplemented by a pension. She found the library had really grown

Jessica was friendly to all, but seemed to prefer male companion-ships. She married four times (twice the marriages were annulled), but she never had a family. Jessica always had a visual defect. She had had eye surgery when she was young. In later years she suffered from glaucoma and though she was gradually loosing her eyesight, she took care of herself at home for years. In January 1955, now blind, Jessica moved into the Sitka Pioneer Home, where she lived to be 95 years of age.

CHAPTER 7

MAIL SERVICE

The mail carriers of the Northland was not always a happy lot, traveling winter through storm and fog on river ice by dog team and in the summer by canoe and Yukon boat, before the horse sled and railroad arrived in the north. In some instances the mail carrier had to eat his dogs to keep alive (Andrews, 1944).

United States Postal Service began in Alaska on July 23, 1867 when a post office was established at Sitka. The first postmaster, John H. Kincad, was later the first governor of Alaska. By 1890, there were eleven post offices. School teachers and traders in outlying Indian villages had to depend on sending an Indian a hundred miles or more to get their mail.

The arrival of the mail-packet was always a great event in the quiet life at the fur trading forts, when month old letters were received. They generally came twice a year, by boat in summer and dog-team in winter, when the journey was made from post to post by some trusty courier. As a rule, the letters were much soiled and worn from frequent handling at the various posts and the thinness of the envelopes was not conducive to secrecy.

Bishop W. C. Bompass of the Church of England who served a lifetime in the north, related an amusing incident. When one courier was hurrying with the mail he broke through the ice. Dogs, man and letters were thoroughly soaked. It was a cold day, so he headed for the shore where the Indian made a good fire, dried his clothes, and then gazed sadly at the wet letters. Finally a thought occurred to him, and taking the soiled epistles out of the envelopes, he stacked them around the fire, near enough to dry, but not to burn. When this was completed to his satisfaction, he began to replace them. But, though well versed in woodland lore, he had never learned to read, so the letters were replaced helter-skelter. Into envelopes addressed to the Bishop went important messages meant only for the company's officers or the love letters sent to men, while the Bishop's letters were disposed of in a similar manner. Thinking he had accomplished a very clever feat, the courier pushed on his way. Upon reaching the fort, he was astonished at the exclamations and excitement of all. Not until the whole matter was explained by the puzzled courier, was its humorous side seen, and then they all had a good laugh.

Meanwhile, indomitable prospectors were making their way into the valley of the Yukon and there were no mail trails. If miners wished to get a letter out of the Yukon, they had to pole up the stiff current of the river in a canoe or boat, then cross the Chilkoot Pass to get to Dyea. If miners wanted to get a sled load of mail taken out to Dyea and Juneau, they would pay a 'snit' of gold dust for each letter. A snit, all a miner could hold between his thumb and forefinger, was counted as a dollar. The value varied greatly since some of the old timers could hold a lot of gold between their and forefinger, was counted as a dollar. The value varied greatly since some of the old timers could hold a lot of gold between their broad thumb and equally broad forefinger.

In 1895 the Canadian government decided to dispatch mail to Dawson from Skagway. Captain Bill Moore, a big burly 73 year old German sourdough, was selected. He started early and crossed the range in the spring of 1896, went down the river and delivered his mail. He then took a steamer to St. Michaels and returned to Victoria, B.C., where he got another load of mail. He made his way back to Circle City, thus completing the first two successful official mail deliveries over the Upper Yukon.

FIRST MAILSLED THROUGH EAGLE
Courtesy: Eagle Historical Society

In 1899, the White Pass and Yukon Railroad was built from Skagway to Whitehorse. Sternwheelers began to operate regularly on the Yukon River and winter sled roads were cut through the wilderness for a cross country snow road. The call, "Make Way for the Royal Mail" rang out regularly in the northern wilderness.

Poor mail service for the miners of the Upper Yukon was one of their continuous complaints. A contract for a service along the river was given, but the immense distances, the inexperience of the contractor, the difficulty of procuring the supplies, all combined with the severity of the weather, to delay the accomplishment of a regular mail route. Low postal rates were one bargain enjoyed by Alaskans. While the first class letter rate was two cents, the federal postal officials estimated it cost at least 50 cents to get each of those letters into the Yukon Valley.

BEN DOWNING
-1906

Big Ben Downing was the man who established the first mail route
down the Yukon in 1899, from Dawson to Nome. He was a typical
frontiersman of the west and north. Like several other outstanding
characters of the Yukon, he was a state of Maine man, tall, sinewy
and stolidly enduring of cold and fatigue. Leaving his Maine home
early in life, he traveled through Texas and ended up in Montana,
where he remained until discovery of gold in the Black Hills lured
him to South Dakota. When the news of the Klondike drifted down
from the North, the call appealed to his roving and adventurous
spirit. He headed for the new diggings and after he arrived, looked
for an opening.

The discovery of gold at Nome in 1899 called attention to the need
of a mail route. Downing, not striking anything very rich at
Dawson, soon secured a Star Route contract to carry the mail
between Dawson and Nome. He began at once to explore the 1500 long
miles of nearly undeveloped stretch of river from Dawson to Nome on
the Bering Sea. He began the work of building cabins to shelter his
carriers every twenty miles. He surveyed for cut-offs, to reduce
the distance by cutting off the bends, and secured teams of hardy
dogs to make the run over the rough ice of the river and through
the winter snows at a temperature sometimes as low as seventy
degrees below zero.

Late in the fall the jamming of ice at intervals and drifting ice
in between in the swift, uneasy flow of the current, makes the
river treacherous. Yukon steamers had already begun to hunt for
their winter quarters. Downing went down the river in a rowboat.
About a day's travel from Circle City, was a roadhouse kept by Old
Man Webber. He was noted for his uproarious disposition, and the
poor quality of his grub. It was said that one could tell how many
teams had passed by from the rings on his bean pot. When Downing
was doing his preliminary survey, it seems someone with a practical
joker's penchant proceeded him, and knowing Webber's irascible
disposition, informed the old man that Downing intended to place a
shelter cabin at his place. This, he said, would constitute a claim
for the land.

Planning to stop for a meal at Webber's roadhouse, Downing and his
assistants innocently arrived on the scene. As they approached,
Webber, shotgun in hand greeted them from the bank of the river.
"You can't stop here!" he shouted waving his gun in the air. "I've
known for a long time the Northern Commercial Company wanted to get
this place. You keep out of here." Downing and his group moved on,
to within about 20 miles above Circle, where they located a
shelter. But Downing never forgot Webber.

A year or two later, traveling back up the line, Downing stopped
over night at Webber's place. Webber lodged him in a bunk in the

rear of the house. Webber had another custom he was noted for. He
used to run out into the snow if he heard a sled come by, to invite
the driver in. This night he heard the sound of sleigh bells on
the trail, and as was his custom, hurried out in his long johns to
stop the traveller. Downing slipped out of bed, and pulled the
latch string on the door bar inside. When Webber returned and
attempted to open the door, he failed. He fumbled and fumed. He
yelled to Downing to open the door. Ben snored. Webber ran around
the house and pounded on the window by Ben's bunk, yelling at him
to open the door. He was freezing; it was about thirty below.
Finally, Ben heard. "What's the matter?" he asked sleepily. "Open
the door, I can't get in" yelled Webber. Ben answered, "OH,
nothing's the matter with the door. Go back and try again." While
Webber stamped around to the back of the road house, Ben jumped out
of bed and poked the latch string through the slot, then jumped
back into his bunk. When Webber entered the room, Ben grouched,
"Didn't I tell you! There's nothing wrong with the door." He had
gotten even with Webber.

Ben seldom got mad himself, but one night he arrived at Rampart
boiling. Someone had stolen his stove at a shelter camp, and when
he had come in after a stormy day, cold and tired, he found no
place to build a fire. He nearly perished of the cold. The rule of
the old timers was to leave the makings for a quick fire, and
stealing a stove was an unpardonable sin. It was the evil of the
Cheechako.

Ben was not only a lover of dogs, but was also an authority on good
ones; he was always ready to buy a good dog or to make a trade. He
had a dog corral near Dawson where he kept over a hundred of his
faithful animals. Running the mail line through the wilderness was
not a small undertaking and gathering the huskies for the drive was
difficult.

Mail carriers were not employees of the U. S. Postal Service, but
were private contractors who bid for the season's mail contract.
Early carriers could expect to get one dollar per letter delivered
and a good commission on the gold they carried. Later, competition
drove the bids down and the carriers got smaller gain for their
efforts.

By 1900, Downing carried passengers and mail, usually using a four
horse bob-sled stage from Dawson to Eagle in the winter. Below
Eagle the drivers teams were dogs, made up of 8 to 10 hitched
tandem. Passengers were obliged to run at the handlebars and were
permitted to ride only in case they gave out, or the mail was
especially light and the trail conditions were excellent. The load
averaged 100 pounds per dog. The dogs were fed only at night. When
the mail team reached the station at the end of the day's run, the
driver unhitched the team and turned all the dogs except the leader
loose to nestle for themselves. The leader, parka, gloves and whip
were taken into the roadhouse. The leader was placed under the bunk

DOWNING'S STAGE LINE 1900
Courtesy: Eagle Historical Society

and the wet garments hung on the best wires around the stovepipe. The driver was given the best seat at the table, first service of hot cakes in the morning and the best bunk at night. All other vehicles were required by U. S. law to give the right of way to mail teams, thus making the mail driver the most important personage on the trail and in the roadhouse (Wickersham, 1938:135).

One winter while carrying the mail with a dog team, Downing ran into a hole in the ice in the Yukon River. The side bars of a dog sled usually terminate in two curved handles, much like the handles of a plow, to which the driver may hold as he runs behind his team. The dogs saw the danger in time to sheer off, but the sled toppled partly into the water, dragging Downing into the river. His dogs, seeing him in distress, were inclined to turn and come to him, but being vigorously urged on they pulled the sled and their master so that by their help he was able to raise himself out of the water, from which he emerged without his cap or mittens, drenched from

95

head to foot. He was several miles from a roadhouse and a less determined man would have frozen stiff in a few minutes. He urged his dogs with all his might and ran at his top speed, knowing that his life depended upon this activity. It was one of those beautiful clear Arctic nights when the mercury crawls down in the bulb and stays there. The temperature was probably about 60 degrees below. His clothes froze so stiff they hindered his running, but he struggled on. Finally reaching the roadhouse, he dashed inside and called for help. His clothes were cut off as rapidly as possible. His face, nose and ears were badly frozen and his feet were almost solid. In a short time he was dressed in dry and warm clothing. With his blistered and swollen feet, he prepared to continue his journey, refusing the roadhouse keeper's urging to remain. He insisted on continuing on to Dawson so that the mail would be delivered on time. As he hobbled into the post office at Dawson, his footsteps were marked with blood.

After the mail was delivered, he was taken at once to the hospital where the doctors decided that his feet were so badly frozen it would be necessary to amputate them. Downing heard this conclusion and he quietly asked some one to hand him his revolver. They hesitated as they thought he might be contemplating suicide, but when he assured them that he had no such intention, they gave it to him. He put it under his pillow, and laid down. "Now," he said, "go ahead and fix up them feet the best you can, but let me tell you that if I wake up and find you fellows have cut them off, I am going to shoot the man that did it. Them feet and me are goin' together; if I live I have use of them, if I can't have them I don't want to live. Now, go ahead." The result was that the ends of several of his toes were trimmed off and the old mail-carrier was not quite as agile as he used to be, but he walked comfortably on two feet. While in the hospital and unable to carry the mail, Downing lost his contract in the United States; with greater appreciation of his remarkable loyalty, the Dominion Government continued his contract to carry the royal mail between Eagle and Dawson (McLean, 1905:89).

The Northern Commercial Company took over the mail run on the United States side of the border; they also took over Downing's dog teams and shelter cabins. The last time Alaskans saw Ben Downing, he was standing on the bank of the Yukon, with a monster of a husky, fore-paws on Ben's shoulder, trying to lick his face. Between dodges to miss the dog's tongue, Ben managed to gasp, "I always did love my dogs." Ben died in January, 1906, in a hospital in San Francisco where he had gone to get rid of the Indian's bullet which he had carried since his days in South Dakota.

Elie Verreau was one of Ben Downing's carriers who took the mail from Dawson to Eagle, making the trip every two weeks. Elie, of French Canadian descent, was one of the best river men at that time. On one trip, carrying fourteen sacks of mail in a Peter-borough canoe, he ran into an ice jam at Coal Creek. The canoe and mail went under the ice cakes. Elie made it ashore but he lost all of the mail sacks plus two pieces of registered mail. One of the mail sacks was found the following spring 180 miles down the river nearly buried in the sand and gravel. One of the pilots of the N.C. Co was making his way along the banks of the river trying to figure out the channels to be used for the coming season. Seeing some rough cloth sticking above the sands, he cut it open, reached inside and pulled out a handful of water soaked letters. He reported the incident to the nearest post office and was promptly arrested for breaking into U.S. mail. After a long debate he finally escaped going to jail.

                         JOHN B. POWERS
                              -1944

John Powers was born near Winona, Minnesota. He became an engineer
on the Northern Pacific Railroad on the run from Missoula, Montana
to Idaho and later went to Indiana and worked on the Wabash Line.
From there he enlisted in the Army Engineers, and served in the
Philippines.

He came to Alaska in 1899 to build a sawmill for the Army, working
as a civilian employee. In 1900, he quit the army and went into the
wood cutting business. With a steam-engine saw outfit, he cut cord
wood for both Fort Egbert and the steamboats, in partnership with
Bert Bryant from 1900-1905. He also freighted with horses,
establishing a regular route between Eagle, Fortymile, Jack Wade,
and Chicken, and had a store and post office at Chicken. He held
the mail contract between Eagle and Chicken for 30 years (1908-
1939), then lost it to the airlines.

In June 1906, John's sister, Mrs. J.E. Stevens moved to Eagle to
keep house for him. She was a widow with two young children,
Marjorie and Bud. Marjorie remembered her uncle as a quiet man.
She said her uncle seemed to have something to do with everything
in Eagle. When men came to see him about business, he would listen
quietly and then give his yes or no. After Fort Egbert was
abandoned, there were only two children left in the Eagle School,
so it was closed. The Stevens left on the last boat in September of
1910 so the children could attend school (EHS Archives,
1910:Powers).

No wonder it seemed to a small girl that John Powers had something
to do with everything in Eagle, as he was always active in
community and political affairs. He was elected to the Eagle City
Common Council almost every year from 1902-1932. He served as Mayor
for so many years he lost count, and also as Magistrate and School
Tax Collector. He was the election Judge intermittently from 1909-
1932. He was elected to the Eagle School Board many of those years.
As overwhelming as all of this involvement might seem, it was not
uncommon for a concerned resident to serve in many capacities.

Powers was appointed Deputy U.S. Marshal at Eagle for eight years
under the Wilson administration. In that capacity he had to make
frequent trips to the Fortymile and Seventymile mining areas. His
monthly reports were well written and very informative.

He was active in politics and was a charter member of the
Jefferson-Jackson Democratic Club in Eagle. He served as a district
and divisional chairman of the Democratic Party for fifteen years.
He was a delegate to Democratic National Conventions in New York
and in Houston, Texas. John Powers was elected Territorial Senator
from Eagle, the 4th Division, in 1935 and 1937. As senator he
traveled around his district, to keep his constitutents informed of

the business of the Territory.

John married Edith Simon in September, 1915 in Dawson. They had been long time friends, as Mrs. Simon had first moved to Fort Egbert in 1901 with her husband, Master-Sgt. Simon and their four small children. The Simons were later divorced and Mrs. Simon had returned to Eagle with her teenage children.

EDITH & JOHN POSERS
Courtesy: Kershaw Collection, EHS

Mrs. Powers was an excellent housekeeper, cook and hard worker. For a period, the Powers took in boarders as well as boarding John's employee. Besides their comfortable home in Eagle City, the Powers had a large red barn for the livestock, complete with a blacksmith shop. In addition to their freighting horses, they kept other livestock and farming equipment. John planted many acres of oats and cut wild grass. Edith helped care for the livestock to the best of her knowledge. She took pity on them and melted snow for drinking water and gave them extra food. Edith used to wash the heavy, bloody horse blankets by hand.

Edith did not socialize with many of the other women in town. She was known for her course language and loud voice, more fitting a teamster or freighter. While John had an easy slow disposition, Edith was prone to fits of anger. Some of John's best employees left after they were the recipient of some of her tirades. Edith not only maintained the family home, but also kept the line cabin at Liberty Creek which John used along his freighting trail to Chicken. He had given it to her as a wedding present. Every summer she walked the thirty miles to Liberty Creek to clean up the cabin, wash the bedding and brush out for the yard. She was happiest in this isolated spot which she called her summer home, preferring it to living in Eagle.

Edith's youngest son, Henry, returned to Eagle in 1918 and worked for John carrying freight and mail to Chicken with the horses. These were happy days for Edith, as she was a warm mother who loved her children, and kept her language and temper under control around them. Henry was engaged to be married and his fiance was enroute to Eagle, when he was drowned while crossing the Fortymile River with a team of horses in June 1923. This was such a shock to Edith, that she never fully recovered and thereafter suffered from long periods of despondency.

John did not like to leave Edith for long periods of time in her despondent mental condition. Prior to leaving for the National Democratic Convention in New York in 1924, he made arrangements with Edith's daughter Patsy, to spend the winter in Eagle with her mother. Patsy was now married and was accompanied by her husband and small son. That spring her second son was born in the Dawson hospital on April 8, 1925.

Edith was never a part of John's political life. To her fell the task of remaining at home and taking care of all the chores. During the long cold dark lonely winters, she worried constantly about the men out on the trail. In December 1936, John had lost two horses when he broke through the ice on the Fortymile River and was barely able to save himself. Power's freighters had a outstanding reputation for punctuality. One very cold day, Edith walked out American Creek carrying the mail bag to meet the freighting team. She continued walking all night and by the time she met the team, she had frozen her feet. She was flown to Fairbanks for surgery and lost toes from both feet. John brought her home to Eagle on April 13, 1937.

In 1938, Edith had a "breakdown" and was admitted to Morningside Hospital for the mentally ill in Portland, Oregon on March 13th. Following her discharge and return home on March 10, 1939, she used to tell her neighbors, she was the only sane person in Eagle; she had the papers to prove it. During the winter of Edith's hospitalization, John wrote that he was lonely, but was caring for himself and the horses though his physical strength and stamina had lowered considerably in recent years. Having lost the mail contract to Chicken in 1937, he had been concentrating on mining at Dome Creek. He had received these mining claims in payment of overdue freighting bills. John continued to make improvements at Dome creek and was hydraulic mining with giants. Even so, his cleanup gold never paid the annual operating expenses and he had to maintain himself on his veteran's pension ($30 month.) He continued working, waiting for the year when he would hit a rich gold area. After returning from Oregon, Edith joined him at Dome Creek, where she cooked for the mining crew. When she was finished cooking, she chopped up all the sluice boxes and burned them and panned the ashes looking for residual gold.

Edith's mental condition worsened over the years and she was again admitted to Morningside Hospital on February 25, 1943. She was there when she learned from an Alaska newspaper that her husband, John, had died on February 15, 1944 in a Fairbanks hospital from cirrhosis of the liver, although he had never been a drinking man. Edith was not quite 74 years old and had been married to John for almost 30 years.

John's will read that Edith was to receive all his income after the debts were paid, as long as she lived. Edith's health improved and she was released from the hospital, but was never permitted to live in her Eagle home or her beloved Liberty Creek summer cabin, as the court would not give her the property titles, nor permit her to use the buildings. Edith lived to be 98 years old and the Power's Estate was still in the hands of the administrator at the time of her death.

ADOLPH (ED) BIEDERMAN
1869-1945

Three generations of Biedermans have lived in Eagle and made major contributions to the community. It all started with Ed, an European immigrant. Adolph Biederman was born in Bohemia, near the Austrian border on September 19, 1869. He came to America when he was fourteen years old and obtained his citizenship papers while in New York. He was a traveler, going first to Cuba, then San Francisco and on to Nome in 1900.

Ed Biederman, as his friends called him, worked for the Northern Commercial Company (NCO) as a trouble shooter, traveling where ever he was needed. He refused to be a manager of any of the stores. When the NCO was awarded the mail contract for the Yukon River, Ed started delivering mail for them. In 1912, they gave him the mail run from Eagle to Circle.

At Circle, Ed met Bella Roderick, daughter of the chief at Medicine Lake, who was known as "Princess." Ed and Bella were married in September, 1916 and moved to Charlie Creek where they built a cabin. Their daughter, Nellie, was born at Circle on July 25, 1917 but the family moved back to Charley Creek for the winter. They had quite a load when they moved, even the old treadle sewing machine. When they left Circle that fall, Ed lined the boat all the way up the river, while Bella guided from the boat.

In 1918, Ed moved his family into Eagle for the winter where their son, Charlie, was born while they were living in Hillard's house. In 1922, they bought their large Eagle home from Mrs. Mae Collins, adding more rooms on as the family grew.

Ed carried the mail during the winter months and the sternwheelers delivered it during the summer. Though the Biederman family wintered in Eagle, they moved down to their fish camp at Charlie Creek each summer. Ed used a large fish wheel which had twelve foot baskets and dipped eight feet into the river. He often handled 150-170 large King Salmon in one 24 hour period. One year with two wheels, he caught 400 salmon in a 24 hour period. He had to stop the wheel for two days to take care of the fish. After cleaning each fish, they were hung to dry. He used five 20'x20' canvas tarps over the drying racks and had three fires to provide smoke. He had eighteen double deck rows with 100 fish to a row, so he could hang 3600 fish to dry. At the end of the summer he bundled the fish up in eighty pound bales which sold for fifteen cents per pound to dog mushers down the river. The fish racks were taken down each fall and rebuilt each spring. Besides fishing, the Biedermans often boarded 60 dogs each summer at the fish camp. Twenty-four of them were their own. Each fall the family returned to Eagle on a sternwheeler, with the dogs and fish bales on the barge.

While carrying the winter mail from Eagle to Circle, a distance of

162 miles, Ed mushed 4200 miles behind huskies every winter. He had
cabins every 25 miles along his route. Sometimes he would make it
to one cabin in four hours, but it could take him as long as 18
hours depending on the weather. When the temperature was lower than
minus 40 degrees, it was almost impossible to travel as the sled
runners stuck in the grooves in the trail.

BIEDERMAN'S MAIL SLED
Courtesy: Eagle Historical Society

The mail contract called for thirteen round trips each winter. It
took six days from Eagle to Circle where they rested one day and
then six days back to Eagle. They met the Fort Yukon mail sled
every two weeks. During one four year period, Ed did not have the
mail run as he was underbid by Johnny Palm of Circle.

In 1925 Ed froze his feet. That fall while returning to Eagle on
the sternwheeler from his fish camp, eight of his dogs, including
his dependable leader, had drowned. When cable on the barge broke
loose, the barge submerged and turned completely over, floating
down river bottom up, drowning the dogs. While using new dogs in
his team, Ed went through some overflow on the river. He didn't
stop to change his footwear and froze his feet. After 25 years in
the north, Ed said he knew better and blamed only himself. He had
to have the fore-part of both feet amputated by Dr. Burke at the
Fort Yukon Hospital. After the surgery he wore regular shoes in the
summer with phonograph springs in the toe of the shoes to keep them
flat. In winter he wore three pairs of socks with the toes stuffed
full of rabbit fur. Over these he wore his moccasins.

103

The accident impaired the circulation in Ed's feet, so he was no longer able to carry the winter mail. His oldest son, Horace, left school at fourteen years of age, to take over the mail run. Later his younger brother, Charlie helped him.

Ed ordered a beautiful large dog sled for the mail route in 1934 from Charlie May at Rampart for $50. It was made out of birch and held together with babiche. The birch runners didn't hold up, so hickory shoes were put on the runners. They used seven to eight dogs on this large sled, which was used for four years. 1936 was a bad winter. It was very cold with lots of snow and the Biedermans lost a lot of their good dogs. In 1938, they lost the mail contract to the Airlines, thus ending the days of dog mushing the mail from Eagle to Circle.

ED & BELLA BIEDERMAN
Courtesy: Eagle Historical Society

Ed used a horse bob-sled for hauling wood, pulling it with fourteen to sixteen dogs. He hauled one cord of green wood with each load. One winter he hauled 78 cords. The Biedermans always had large stacks of firewood in their yard, each piece cut an exact length and piled very neatly.

In 1933, at 68 years of age, Ed was described as tough as nails. He was a small man, brown as leather and wiry, who walked with a thump-thump. He still spoke with an accent. Biederman had come to Alaska at the turn of the century, had never made a trip outside and never intended to.

Ed had a good sense of humor and enjoyed conversing. His conversation was heavily sprinkled with cuss words. In his later life, he didn't drink or smoke. He quit drinking in mid-life because he had gotten drunk and missed collecting $190 that someone owed him. He quit smoking because it hurt his wind. He began to wear a mustache to cover up his bad teeth, but continued wearing it after getting false teeth. He said it frosted over in the wintertime and protected his mouth. As he got older, Ed's health began to fail. He was under a doctor's care when he died at home in 1945.

Biederman's eldest son, Horace, owned and operated a general store in Eagle. His wife had died of peritonitis leaving him with two small children, Horace Jr. and Florence. After her mother's death, Florence lived with her grandmother, Bella, who raised her. Bella continued to live in the Biederman home with Flossie after Ed died. It wasn't until she became crippled, that she moved in with her son, Horace.

Bella was a remarkable Indian lady. She had a good sense of humor and loved to tell her children stories of her early married life. Ed and his wife got along well. They were both proud of their growing family, raising seven children. Ed had taught Bella to speak English, how to cook the foods he liked and how to keep house. She taught herself to play pinochle and loved to play cards. When no one was around to play cards with her, she enjoyed solitaire. She joined in the town's activities, even working in the library though she had never learned to read. She was a good dancer and loved to attend the many dances held at the Improved Order of Redmen's Lodge. For years, she tended the wood fire in the town's public well-house all winter. Bella died on October 20, 1967 at an estimated age of 88 and was buried in the Eagle City cemetery. Her birthdate had never been recorded, but Bella had been told she was born when the leaves were coming out, so her family always celebrated her birthday on Mother's Day.

Bella had left her Indian customs behind her, never talking about them or passing them on to her children. She lived in a white community in the same style as the other ladies. During this period, any Indian lady married to a white man forfeited all rights to special Indian privileges for herself and her children, which included health, education, and social services. The children attended the public school in Eagle City through the 8th grade. As the children were growing, one daughter said they did not feel accepted by the Indian or white communities, but they always had the support of a close loving family.

In 1995, the family donated one of Ed's dog sleds used on his mail run, to the Smithsonian Museum in Washington, D.C. where it can be viewed in the U. S. Postal Service exhibit. The site of the Biederman fish camp at Charlie River is privately owned and in 1997 continues to serve as a check-point for the Yukon Quest International dog-sled race.

PERCY DE WOLFE
-1951

Percy DeWolfe, a Canadian mail carrier, delivered the mail from Dawson to Eagle for 35 years. He was a beloved character in Eagle and is frequently mentioned in its history. He was born on February 15, 1877 in Nova Scotia. He arrived in the Yukon in June 1898 with his friend, Peter Anderson, after a long hazardous trip down the Pelly and Yukon Rivers in a small boat. They established a profitable fishing business during the summer and a freighting business to the Fortymile area during the winter. They built a road house at Sixteenmile River. Two years later they constructed the Halfway House (halfway between Dawson and Fortymile), where Percy lived many years. In 1903, Percy and his partner stampeded to

PERCY DEWOLFE AND DAUGHTERS AT HALFWAY HOUSE
Courtesy: Eagle Historical Society

Fairbanks, but returned to Dawson in 1904. They resumed their fishing, freighting, hunting and woodcutting business. DeWolfe and Anderson married two native sisters. Jesse DeWolfe bore six children at Half-way House. She died in 1917 and Percy never remarried.

In 1915 Percy took over Elie Verreau's contract to deliver the mail between Dawson City and Eagle, Alaska. Between 1908-1915 Elie carried the mail summer and winter at the constant annual price of $9,000. The American government paid for part of the cost of this service, accounting for $1,038 of the annual total contract. Verreau's contract at a flat rate was unusual as it was more customary for a mail contract to be let for a specified sum per trip.

When DeWolfe entered a direct contract with the federal government, he was hired by the latter method and contracted to take only the winter mail. In the summer months, mail went by regular steamer, saving the Canadian and American governments considerable sums of money. Initially DeWolfe agreed to make the 204 mile round trip once a week for $125 and earned only $4,000 for each of his first two contract years. Afterwards when he contracted for $160 per trip to make three trips a month and his total annual fee often fell below that of his initial years. Nevertheless DeWolfe frequently carried freight and passengers on his rounds, as the requirement of his contract did not force the total suspension of his private freighting business.

Each fall DeWolfe supplied his small way stations and cabins at Halfway House, Fortymile, Midway Point and Eagle with 30 tons of hay, oats, dogfood and groceries. The winter contract left him free to pursue summer interest, freighting along the river and fishing commercially with a fish wheel, drying the fish and selling it in Dawson. In the early 1920's, he tried his hand at fox farming and in 1927, he did some silver mining in the region of the Halfway House.

Percy's 102 mile long mail route took eight days, four days each way. His endurance of winter trails and his narrow escapes while carrying the mail, spring and fall, on perilous ice floes were legendary. The mails arrived by horse, dogsled, motor launch or on Percy's back. No wonder they called him the 'Iron Man of the North'. Typical of the news stories about Percy, are the following.

●MAIL CARRIER BREAKS THROUGH THE ICE.....Three horses and sleigh were sucked down by river current and lost.....all mail saved.....DeWolfe hiked to Dawson with lower river mail over his shoulder.

●LAUNCH.....HEAVY ICE.....ABANDONS BOAT AT FANNINGS.....Walking back to Dawson, DeWolfe fell from the bluff below Fortymile River ...... walking along the bluff in stocking feet to prevent slipping, he suddenly tumbled down 100 feet, dazed, but had no broken bones.

●OVERDUE ONE WEEK IN FEBRUARY.....January had been the toughest time ever, but DeWolfe turned up O.K.

Percy's arrival was eagerly awaited by the isolated prospectors at Eagle and Fortymile. The sight of Percy mushing into view would often bring out an excited crowd. On one occasion the people of Eagle, upon hearing that Percy had brought one of his daughters and her family, hurriedly staged a dance in their honor. The city hall, which had been closed for many years, was opened, the floor polished, the chairs dusted and the band struck up with a bang. Everyone had a wonderful time.

DeWolfe was as reliable as the sun in a climate where such reliability was a monumental achievement. He not only brought the mail but in isolated way stations he proved a hardy link with the outside world, freighting cargo that ranged from 80 cases of cream, to plants of that most delectable Dawson celery to a genuine hogswallow bath tub. To the people along his route, he brought news of the condition of the river and trails, often lifesaving information. He carried passengers as well as freight in and out of the remote regions of the Yukon River. On more than one occasion he brought a sourdough miner to Dawson for medical attention, delivered a mail order bride to an isolated mine and took a young girl on the round trip for a winter view of the border. During the 1937 flood, Percy rescued John Fanning when his roadhouse had been swept away.

After 35 years of consecutive mail service, logging over 100,000 miles, he retired in 1950 at 73 years of age. In Dawson, DeWolfe was honored by His Majesty, King George V of England, and presented with a silver medal to be worn in commemoration of their Majesty's Silver Jubilee. He died in 1951.

An INTERNATIONAL DOG TEAM MILE RUN between Dawson City and Eagle City was started in 1977 to honor the legendary mail carrier, Percy DeWolfe. The dog race has continued as an annual event and attracts much attention in the Upper Yukon area.

CHAPTER 8

AGRICULTURE

When the first white men settled in the Upper Yukon, many of them added variety to their food supply by cultivating gardens. A few even supplemented their income by selling their home grown vegetables. The traders usually had large gardens. Jack McQuesten was a successful gardener at Fortymile. He plowed his ground with a team of dogs. Later he trained a pair of young moose to the harness and plowed with them. Horses and cows were not introduced into the Upper Yukon until the U. S. Army and Klondike miners brought them. The Indians called the animals 'McKinley Moose'.

MOOSE USED TO PLOW GARDENS
Courtesy: University of Alaska, Fairbanks Archives

As early as 1885, in the course of his military reconnaissance, Lt. Allen noted that lettuce, radishes, turnips, beans, peas, potatoes, carrots and possibly buckwheat and barley could be raised through the middle and upper Yukon and Tanana Valleys (Allen, 1885:411). This slowly sparked some federal interest in Alaskan agriculture and Congress appropriated $5,000 in 1897 for the Secretary of Agriculture to investigate and report to Congress on the agricultural resources and capabilities of Alaska and the feasibility of establishing experimental stations in the District.

The Secretary of Agriculture requested Dr. Sheldon Jackson to investigate the Yukon Valley. He reported, "While Alaska will never be an agricultural state in the same sense in which that term is understood in the Mississippi Valley, it does have agricultural capacity much in advance of the public sentiment of the country" (Georgeson, 1899).

Six miles below Circle City, a good garden had been established by a gentleman who supplied the miners with fresh vegetables. Mr. R. Wilson cut cord wood for the steamers. When his clearings were large enough to let the sun reach the ground, he would loosen the soil between the roots and stumps and sow turnip seed. In 1896, he marketed 3,000 pounds of turnips, receiving fifteen cents a pound.

In 1900, Professor C.C. Georgeson visited the Yukon Valley, in behalf of the Department of Agriculture, with plans to interest settlers in some agricultural work, and, if possible, to start some experiments in growing vegetables and cereals in private gardens. At Eagle, he found several promising gardens. Mr. O.H. Walters had a fine potato patch and Father Monroe had a large garden at the Catholic Mission which contained nearly all the hardy vegetables, but the largest garden was at Fort Egbert. There he found potatoes, carrots, peas, wax beans, lettuce, radishes, cabbage and cauliflower, all doing well. They also had small patches of barley and oats well headed out. A settler in the valley on the other side of the river had a small field of oats and some barley doing well. In the natural meadows, the grass grew luxuriantly wherever the moss was destroyed so that it could get a foothold. Residents requested that an experimental station be located at Eagle, but Mr. Georgeson did not feel justified in selecting the somewhat isolated site on the boundary, which was not representative of the vast interior. He did distribute seed to all who wanted it, and one of the settlers agreed to grow some of the leading kinds of grain the next year as an experiment, for which he was supplied with seed. Rampart was selected as the site for the Department of Agriculture experimental station.

Free seed distribution was regarded as legitimate experimental work. The recipients became cooperators with the experimental stations and the distribution of seeds stimulated the development of agriculture. There were soon gardens in hundreds of places where there otherwise would have been none. Distribution of seed also had the effect of encouraging the natives to start gardens with the assistance of missionaries, teachers, or well disposed white men. Brief directions were sent out with the seeds for the benefit of those who had no experience, and correspondence on the subject of the cultivation of crops of every kind was solicited.

The soldiers at Fort Egbert not only raised large vegetable gardens, but also grain. Sgt. Woodfield told about the military gardeners popularity. When there wasn't anything else exciting to do at the Fort, the soldiers had a habit of dropping in on their two gardeners, Micky Welsh and John Purcell, to insist on their producing something new in the line of food. Those lads didn't live with the rest of the soldiers in the barracks. They had a little cabin of their own in one corner of their garden. They had a cook stove and could cook up a fancy meal for visitors, if you were lucky enough to be one of their pals. Of course, everybody kept on good terms with Micky and Johnny. They grew turnips as big as a three gallon bucket. Everything grew to a huge size right out in the open except tomatoes, which had to be raised under glass.

Early Eagle residents depended on horses for their transportation and work, so they put up a lot of natural hay from the meadows around Eagle. Each spring the fields were burned off and in the fall they cut the wild hay with a mowing machine. The City of Eagle rented out the town lots which were hay meadows, especially those near Buckeye Creek. They also rented the school reserve acres to raise grain. John Powers, who kept a string of horses for his transportation business, set up a hay meadow camp each fall and hired five mowers and a cook. His camp was on the hillside behind American Creek and Mission Creek.

Early residents remember that many of the vacant blocks and lots in Eagle were gardened, not only for their personal use, but also to sell; there was a commercial demand up and down the river, for all the potatoes and other vegetables available, selling at a good price. One day in 1918, August Fritsch, a banner farmer, made a shipment of five tons of potatoes to Fort Yukon. All of the gardens had to be fenced, as the horses had the run of the town.

PETER LUNDEEN
1860-1922

Peter Lundeen was the only full time farmer around Eagle between 1900 and 1920. He had arrived in Eagle in 1898 and had staked a homestead across the river from Eagle City. He made more money selling eggs and milk and vegetables to the citizens of the Far North than he ever had in the days he spent digging for gold.

Lundeen was born in Sweden February 20, 1860. Like many Scandinavians caught up in the European depression, he made his way to America as a young man and became a naturalized citizen in 1886.

PETE LUNDEEN WITH KATY & PATSY SIMON
Courtesy: Kershaw Collection, EHS

Lundeen was a large likeable man known by the locals as the "Big Swede." He was a hard worker and built his log house and log barn with double walls of logs. He cleared many acres on his farm where he grew large fields of grain. He had a large fish wheel near his farm, and used many of the fish for fertilizer in his gardens. He cut wild hay on the Eagle meadows for his cattle.

In 1903, Lundeen reported that three grains, wheat, barley and oats, had matured perfectly. The wheat reached a height of 5' and the oat 5 2/3' and the barley 5'. He had five acres in cultivation for his garden, on which the turnips and cabbage did well.He raised 100 sacks of potatoes on three-fourths of an acre of ground. He had three cows, two calves and several pigs. He had just completed his double log barn and planned to have a large silo by fall.

OATS GROWING ON LUNDEEN FARM
Courtesy: C.L. Andrews Collection

Lundeen used a small rowboat to bring his produce, eggs and milk to
sell at Eagle City. The Army and housewives were steady customers,
anxious to get his fresh goods. He also played the violin for many
of the town's social gatherings. One fall he started across the
river in his boat to play at a dance, but there was so much ice
running in the river, he wound up way down stream before he could
reach the other side. Undaunted, he hiked over the top of the high
Eagle Bluff on the river, so the dance still had live music from
the Big Swede, though a little later than usual.

LUNDEEN'S FARM BUILDINGS 1909
Courtesy: Arthur Knudsen, EHS

One of the soldiers at Fort Egbert, Samuel Woodfill, liked to tell
the following story about Lundeen (Thomas, 1929). "As far as I
know, the only time in his life that Big Swede ever had a bath was
when he fell into the river. At the time, he was rowing a load of
cabbages across from his estate. One of his oars slipped, and when
he tried to grab it, out he went head first into the Yukon. A
fellow on the Eagle side saw his spill and pushed out in a boat,

115

but he couldn't get Pete to start for shore until he had rounded up his vegetables. There's a short growing season in Alaska and cabbages are cabbages. 'Aye tank I bane fish 'em out first,' he kept on saying."

Woodfill continued, "They finally got most of the cabbages and then the man, who had gone to his rescue, brought Pete into the bar room. That was in October, and the old Yukon was about to freeze over. Pete was so cold, his false teeth were doing a shimmy. So we just shot fire water into him until he warmed up. When he finally staggered out the door and went about his peddling, old Pete didn't know whether he was selling cabbages or straw hats."

The years sped by and Lundeen had developed quite a farm, all that one man could handle. But as he got older, he developed chronic nephritis and was no longer able to care for himself. He had to stay forty-three days with John Pierson who provided him room and board and nursing care until his friends could get him into the Pioneer Home in Sitka. He died shortly after his arrival in Sitka, November 22, 1922, at the age of 62 years.

Lundeen had remained a bachelor, but he did have two sisters who had moved to the United States. Tom King was appointed adminis-trator of his estate. Unfortunately, Lundeen had never received title to his homestead, but his buildings and land were appraised for $500 and the rest of his estate at $561. He had no money, no income of any kind and had made no will. But the outline of his fields and buildings still remain as evidence of the many years Peter Lundeen spent farming across the river from Eagle.

CHAPTER 9

CHURCHES

Missionaries from major churches arrived in Eagle City shortly after the town was organized. The two earliest ones were the Catholic and Presbyterian Churches, followed shortly by the Episcopalian Church.

CATHOLIC CHURCH

In August 1899, Father Monroe arrived at Eagle to establish a mission. Since there were few Catholics in the town, he was able to spend seven or eight weeks every year visiting the Circle and Fortymile districts as well as to open and operate a small hospital.

Father Monroe was born near Lyons, France on June 2, 1855. He entered the Jesuit Order on Nov. 4, 1874, was ordained a priest on June 24, 1886, and came to America that same year.

In 1893 after spending several years as a missionary among the Indians of Montana, Fr. Monroe was assigned to Alaska. On July 1st he arrived at Holy Cross Mission were he spent the first of his 46 years in Alaska. From 1894 to 1898, he was stationed at Nulato. From that base, he traveled long distances, ministering to the miners as far as Circle City and the Fortymile country. In 1895 he had traveled more than 500 miles alone and on foot in a country where roads and even trails did not exist. During his travels he ministered the sacraments of baptism, marriage and extreme unction to some white people for the first time. On July 2, 1895, sixty miles up the Fortymile River, Father Monroe met Mr. and Mrs. Hubert Day at Miller Creek and baptized their twin boys, born at Ogilvie on the Yukon, on October 13, 1894. They were the first white children born in that part of the Yukon Territory.

The first mining settlement Father Monroe came across was nicknamed 'The Little Ireland.' All of the men, half a dozen, were Irish and Catholic, except for the well-educated civil engineer. Father Monroe received a hearty welcome; the good people never expected to see a priest in their wilderness. They did not think it possible for anyone, especially a priest, to travel alone through such a country. In fact, before leaving Fortymile Post, Father Monroe had tried to hire a Native as a guide, but the Anglican Bishop at the Fortymile Mission had dissuaded his Indians from accepting the offer, so he decided it would be best to travel alone after all.

In 1899 when Father Monroe was placed in charge of the Upper Yukon area, the Fortymile district counted about 1,500 men and Circle had about 600. Eagle City had been established, an Army Fort built adjacent to the city and there was talk of a railroad being built from Valdez to Eagle. The City had great prospects; he decided

Eagle would be a good place for the Catholic Church's headquarters.

FATHER MONROE & ST. FRANCIS XAVIER MISSION, EAGLE CITY
Courtesy: Eagle Historical Society

When Father Monroe arrived in Eagle on August 10th, a Catholic family was in the process of leaving and offered him a site for his mission in the most favorable part of town for $300. The Father accepted the offer as there were also two cabins. The larger cabin 20'x 22' became the residence and chapel. The mission was named St. Frances Zavier. More lots were acquired later for small sums. The Church property eventually comprised of seven lots, each 50'x150'. Most of the ground was turned into a garden which proved to be a great help for the mission. For several years the garden very nearly provided Father Monroe's entire living.

Before the end of the summer in 1899, Father Monroe had been joined by Father Camille, S.J., a French Father who had only been in America a few months. He was full of ambition and zeal, so was greatly disappointed to find himself in a place where there was hardly enough work or resources for one priest. The following summer, he was called to Juneau, leaving Father Monroe alone for four more years.

There were only 50 Catholics at Eagle and the surrounding areas. During the first year there were neither baptisms, marriages nor deaths in the parish. At the end of the first year, receipts from the people of the parish amounted to $151; expenses, not including the cost of the property, amounted to over $1,000.

The most ordinary laborer was paid 75 cents to $1.00 an hour; not having any extra money, Father Monroe had to be his own house-keeper, carpenter and gardener. Yet, he found enough time to go around to help poor sick people. Eagle residents realized that something had to be done for the sick folks and they requested Father Monroe to start a small hospital. In an hour $750 was subscribed and more help promised. Next to Father's cabin was another cabin which he opened for a hospital and operated it for three years. In the fall of 1903, the military hospital was permitted to admit civilian patients, so Father closed his hospital at once. He had cared for thirty men for a total of 730 days.

As a rule the little hospital had few patients during the summer, so Father Monroe would spend two months every year visiting the Catholics of the Fortymile and Circle districts, as he had done in 1895. The spiritual result of these hard trips was far from encouraging. The parish book records for those five years, totaled twelve baptisms, two marriages, five burials and one man received into the church.

In 1903 gold was struck in the Tanana Valley and another gold rush was on. Though it was some 350 miles away, Father Monroe considered it part of his district and he was anxious to follow the crowd to organize a Church there. Permission to move was finally received June 21, 1904. The little mission of St. Francis Zavier was closed and Father Monroe moved to Fairbanks.

At the time the Klondike gold strike was attracting so many people, the Presbyterian Church invited the Rev. S. Hall Young, a missionary in South-east Alaska, to go into the Klondike which at that time was thought to be in American territory. He made the dangerous journey over the Chilkoot Pass on foot and down the Yukon River in a small open boat.

During the fall and winter of 1897, he organized the Presbyterian Church in Dawson and helped to establish a hospital. During the summer of 1898 he traveled down the Yukon River and visited the mining camps as far as Rampart. When he returned to the states he urged the Home Mission Board to send missionaries into the Yukon Valley.

Rev. Kirk, a graduate of the Princeton Theological Seminary, had been the minister at a Philadelphia Presbyterian Church for seventeen years when Mr. Young visited them and asked if they would accept a missionary assignment to Eagle City on the Yukon. When it was determined they would go, there was one major question to be answered. When you are going to a land without any furniture and you are only allowed to take two pieces, what would you take? Mrs. Kirk immediately responded, "We will take our piano and sewing machine." They also packed books and other supplies for a reading room, a hospital outfit, winter clothing, plus a few of the nicer things, such as house silver, fine china and table linen. They also took a small organ donated by their Philadelphia congregation and a church bell from Albany.

During the spring of 1899, Rev. & Mrs. Kirk traveled close to 3000 miles from Philadelphia to Seattle, where they boarded a steamer for Skagway. There they learned that the Chilkoot Trail was closed while a railway was being constructed over the White pass. After waiting two weeks, they paid 25 cents a mile for the 40 mile railway trip over the White Pass to Lake Bennett. They rode the last 22 miles in Canada in an open flat car creeping along the unballasted track. At Bennett they transferred to a steamer bound for Miles Canyon, 100 miles below the Lake, where a transfer was made to a tram car drawn on a wooden track by horse power. The connecting steamer below the Canyon took them to Dawson where they transferred to an American Steamer which took them to Eagle.

When they approached Eagle, it was midnight, but still as light as day. A hundred men stood on the river bank watching the pilot make a landing in the swift current. Several men were waiting for them and each offered the use of their cabin until they found their own. Mrs. Kirk was dismayed at the sight of the log cabins with dirt roofs that sagged in the center. After accepting the use of one cabin, the owner returned to prepare them breakfast. The Kirks were greatly disturbed to learn that men were leaving Eagle instead of

REV. & MRS. JAMES WOOLASTON KIRK, 1902
Courtesy: Eagle Historical Socity

instead of flocking to it. The Kirks announced that in spite of the prospects, they were there to stay and make the best of it. They needed to get a cabin and get settled before the snow flew.

The Kirks finally found a small 15'x18' one room cabin with walls of unpeeled logs and rough board floor, showing big cracks. The roughly joined door did not close tight or fit its jamb and the one small window was covered with white cheese cloth in lieu of netting. The Rev. tried to cheer his wife by saying he would add another room and fix up the cabin so that it would be warm and habitable.

Arrangements were made to hold a service on Sunday. A saloon keeper good naturedly closed his bar and permitted the Kirks to conduct services in his big tent on the river front. The ground was covered with saw-dust, boards supported on boxes were the seats, a table covered with a wolf robe served as the pulpit and the baby organ helped the singers. The singing attracted some who dropped in, and outdoor listeners could hear all that was said. The saloon was reopened as soon as the meeting was closed.

The male choir sang with zest. The Kirks had taken hymnals with them and a number of the congregation remained to rehearse new music for the evening service, which was better attended than the morning one. Many were introduced, and the half dozen women seemed glad to welcome an increase in their number even by one.

After their day of rest, the Kirks had to tackle the bewildering confusion of their little cabin. Boxes containing the piano, church bell, sewing machine, washing machine, books, clothing, stoves and provisions filled the entire floor space, and were piled up as high as one could reach. The Yukon cook stove was placed out of doors under the cabin eaves and protected by canvas from draughts. Mrs. Kirk would now be cooking before the public. She was advised to watch out for the dogs when she was cooking as they were terrible thieves and would snatch a pan of meat right off the hot stove. Just say 'mush' (marche) and the dogs would leave. A tent they had brought from Seattle was set up west of the cabin door as a dining room. A big box turned upside down served as the table but with the linen, china, glass and silver it looked inviting. The Kirks were determined to entertain their generous host and others who had assisted them. The men were good cooks and taught Mrs. Kirk to prepare evaporated and condensed foods and to roast meat in the Yukon oven. Looking at her cuts and scratches, she was determined to learn to open tin cans. The Yukon stove seemed specially designed to burn her fingers.

The cabin was soon brought into some semblance of order. Rev. Kirk began to build an addition to the house, using slabs over the frame building to match the logs of the cabin. Paper and sawdust were put between the studs to keep out the wind. The flooring was planed and covered with building paper over that to have a warm floor as there would be no carpet, at least that year.

During the first summer there were many diversions for the Kirks. The first meeting of the Presbytery was held in Eagle, Alaska July 26, 1899. July 31st a steamer arrived at Eagle with Co. L, Seventh Infantry, U.S.A. The original small detachment of soldiers that had come in under Captain Richardson were glad to be relieved. The officers and families were domiciled in cabins that were convenient. The Kirks assisted the Surgeon and his wife in finding a suitable cabin, hence becoming lasting friends.

A visit by the Hon. John G. Brady, Governor of the Territory, August 5th created quite a stir in the community. The steamboat on which he traveled remained several hours. The mission bell was rung to call the people together and a meeting was held in the open air, the address being from the porch of a cabin on Front Street. Governor Brady was the Kirk's guest for a noonday meal. Linen, china, silver and glass were not wanting, but the crowded little place had no furniture. A beautiful large quilt was hung to conceal the bed. The Governor was looking under the tablecloth to see what kind of a carpenter the preacher was, but Mrs. Kirk readily assured him the box was just temporary and they would have a better table by and by.

When cool weather made the saloon tent uncomfortable for church services, the saloon keeper offered his large cabin without rent as a place for their meetings, though for a time a double row of beer barrels were stored in the same room. Many strong and musical male voices joined in the singing. As the tunes in the Hymnals were new to most of them, a general invitation was given to meet at the Kirk's home on Friday evenings for a singing practice. Thus began the 'musicals' which were held regularly thereafter and became a great pleasure for many.

At first the baby organ was used for the hymns and songs. Before another Sunday went by, the piano was opened, but left in the box, whose front had been taken off. Mrs. Kirk was an accomplished pianist and folks hearing the piano, gathered into the cabin, transforming it into a charmed concert hall, if one's eyes were closed.

Summer slipped away only too fast. There simply was not enough money to build a church edifice that first year, so the Kirks decided to live in one room and use the other for services on Sunday and a public reading room during the week. The first service was held there October 1st. On Thanksgiving a religious service was held in the morning and a musical and literary program in the evening. Refreshments were served though the little Yukon cook stove had freaks of its own and cake baking was not easy. An invitation for a similar gathering at Christmas was accepted at once.

The Kirks soon learned the intricacies, routine and etiquette of an army post and the officers and their wives became good friends. Few of the enlisted men had social privileges beyond the mission and most of them were lonely. The Kirks home became a dropping-in place for all, from the stately military officers to the youngest boy in the garrison; and from tourists fresh from the States to the hardy miner from the creeks. Their home always seemed to have visitors from ten in the morning until late at night. Mrs. Kirk often had to do her household chores while visiting, but she didn't know what to do about washing their clothes. They solved that by getting up at 5 a.m. and washing clothes, so that everything would be cleaned up by the time the visitors began to arrive.

The Nome stampede made a great change in Eagle after January 1900. Some of the finest young men took dogs and sleds, tents and provisions, and set out on the tedious and hazardous journey of nearly 1500 miles in the middle of the winter. The Kirks found it hard to part with them just as their acquaintance was ripening into friendship and helpfulness and their circle was small at best.

During the stampede to Nome, travelers of all descriptions stopped at Eagle, Alaska. It was not unusual to see a dozen dog teams leave the road houses early in the morning, with thirty or forty mushers. One Sunday morning, Rev. Kirk caught the gleam of a bright red fez on the raven locks of an attractive woman whose attitude was reverent and attentive. She remained after the service and frankly told her story. She was from South America and was mushing over the trail to Nome with a man hired to drive her dog team. When asked if she wasn't afraid to travel alone, she replied, "Yes, but I do not fear anything except that I have started too late and the ice may begin to break before I reach Nome. I am strong, have good dogs, plenty of money and we women of the South know how to defend ourselves. I have here a revolver and here a dagger. A friend has taken up claims for us, but he cannot hold them when the rush comes in the summer, and my husband or myself must be there. He is young, ten years younger than I, and has gone to the coast for horses, but I left word. I dared not wait longer, and he must come by boat when the ice breaks. He is a rich man's son, never used to hard work. He cannot stand it as I can, for all my life I have been out of doors, riding everywhere with my father and walking as I wished, but he is frail. I fear only for him."

The lady returned for the evening service but the fez was replaced by a seal skin cap. During the service, she suddenly rushed out of the church, but returned in a few minutes. After the service she explained, "You must pardon my going out. I went for this (producing the fez), much money is sewed in its lining, all hundred dollar bills. I remembered it was in the cabin and feared to lose it." Later the Kirks learned that after many hardships, the lady in the fez had made the perilous journey in safety and was joined by her husband when navigation opened.

Indians of the Takudh dialect were scattered over British North America and Alaska. English missionaries had followed the Hudson Bay Company's settlements and taught the Indians to read their own language, having translated the Bible, prayer and hymn books for their use. The English Bishop was unable to supply a missionary to the Indian village three miles from Eagle and said if Rev. Kirk would take charge of them, he would provide the books needed and an interpreter. A service was arranged for them every Sunday morning and was held in the mission at Eagle with an excellent attendance, even in extreme cold weather. The service of the English Prayer Book was read by the interpreter in the Takudh. The sermon was in

English but interpreted.

The Church of England missionary made an annual visit to Eagle; he held the Sunday service in the village. It was their communion day and about one hundred were present, out of which forty communed. A collection was taken in a tin wash basin and the result was one caribou skin (tanned), two pairs of moccasins, one tablespoon, one dinner plate, two plugs of tobacco, fifty-eight bunches of sulphur matches and $10.25 in cash.

Their first long cold winter finally ended. In June the steamboats began coming down the river from Dawson bringing potatoes, fruit and eggs, but the prices were extremely high. Oranges cost 50 cents each, potatoes 60 cents a pound, and eggs were $1.50 a dozen. When the steamboats began arriving from the Bering Sea in July, the prices became more reasonable.

In 1900 the Yukon Presbytery was to be held in Nome during the summer. Rev. Kirk was sure that his wife would accompany him on this novel 3,000 mile long journey, which would probably take less than four weeks. Mrs. Kirk refused the invitation to accompany her husband as she felt it was necessary to keep the mission open, books and piano accessible and to meet strangers who came on the steamers and wished to know about their work. Since there would be no darkness during the summer, she was not afraid to stay alone.

When asked what she would do on Sundays, she said, "Oh, I can talk to the Indians in the mornings, for few white men rise early enough to come at half past ten, though the Indians walk four miles and are seldom late. They love to sing their own Takudh hymns. Stephen interprets well, and I shall quite enjoy it. There will be no evening service, of course. White people would not want a woman to conduct meetings." The Rev. thought the white people might like song services and meetings after the order of the Christian Endeavor Society. He was right as the young men said they couldn't be neglected and arrangements for evenings were made with the hope that some of the residents or visiting strangers might assist.

The first steamboats which came down the Yukon were so crowded that barges were often connected to accommodate the throngs of gold seekers rushing to Nome. On one of these, the minister was a half reluctant passenger. When the couple bid adieu, little did Mrs. Kirk realize that she wouldn't see her husband again for three months, as a smallpox quarantine kept him in Nome much longer than expected.

Mrs. Kirk did keep things going at the mission. Friends were kind, attentive and sociable. One neighbor took responsibility of ringing the bell for services and took care of the little garden. Another from the military hospital corps arranged the pews and other sittings in the reading room, brought water, cut wood and in general took care of the place. Once the corpsman arrived just in

time to remove a drunken man who "meant no harm, heard a piano and
just dropped in for a spell." There was a standing invitation to
visit the Military Surgeon's wife for breakfast, lunch or dinner.
One of the Lieutenants caught greyling, came to supper and cooked
them
himself to prove that he was an expert cook. Friends brought fish,
wild game, vegetables and fruit.

Sundays were hard but happy days. The Indians with squaws, papooses
and youths were always present in the mornings. Leaders for the
evening meetings were not found, so this duty always fell to the
minister's wife, and hers was the only voice heard in prayer.

EAGLE CHURCH AND MANSE
Courtesy: Eagle Historical Society

Though home folks had considered Mrs. Kirk to be timid, sensitive
and shrinking by nature, she soon found she had more talent than
even she realized which she put to good use in the far northern

frontier. Needless to say, there was a happy reunion when the Rev. returned from Nome.

The Kirk's remained in Eagle for three years (1899-1902). During that time, they built a small church and residence next door. They received word that they should go to the states for a winter's furlough. Though they were homesick for their families, they refused to leave Eagle until a replacement had been found for them. When they learned that Rev. and Mrs. Charles F. Ensign of Iowa were on their way to carry on the work during their absence, they made plans to return to the states.

In their home city, Philadelphia, there were many requests for speeches. Mrs. Kirk had started recording her Alaskan experiences, but she found little time to work on her manuscript. While in Washington following an invitation for a visit and to address meetings, Mrs. Kirk became seriously ill, and died in a few days. Rev. Kirk returned to Alaska serving as a missionary from 1902-1907. He also completed his wife's manuscript which was published in 1935, entitled <u>Pioneer Life in the Yukon Valley.</u>

REV. & MRS. CHARLES L. ENSIGN

Rev. C. F. and Mrs. Ensign were assigned to work at Eagle during the Kirks' winter furlough and arrived there September 4, 1902. Upon learning of Mrs. Kirk's death, the Ensigns were given a permanent appointment to the Eagle station.

The wrote, "Our reading room is open afternoons and evenings. Our home is always open. Many evenings, men, women and the soldier boys come and spend with us. We are always ready to lend the helping hand."

Mrs. Ensign opened a day school for 14 Indian children in the church in town. The first day the teacher armed herself with a black board made of black paper tacked to a board, a box of crayons and a pan full of cookies. The pupils understood not one word of English nor the teacher any of their Indian language. For the first few weeks, the gesticulations were frantic on both sides, but by degrees they reduced themselves to words and finally sentences.

During the July 1903 Yukon Presbytery meeting in Rampart, Rev. Ensign was directed to organize the Indians at Eagle into a Presbyterian church and Mrs. Ensign was recommended to the Women's Board as their special missionary to the Indians at Eagle. The Ensign's gave a lot of attention to the Indians in the village, who numbered 64 in 1902. Most of them had their own cabins which they only lived in during the winter. They hunted and fished and found a ready market for the game. Some were very filthy, while others were more clean in their habits. The people of Eagle City were helpful to the Indians when they were sick or in need. The Army

127

physician attended the natives when they were sick. Rev. Ensign recommended that the government establish a school for the natives and care for the destitute.

Rev. Ensign was active within the community while living in Eagle, participating in both the Improved Order of Red Men fraternity and the Arctic Brotherhood. He also attended City Council meetings and continuously recommended the saloons be closed on Sundays.

The Ensigns remained in Eagle City until 1905. Later the Presbyterian Mission at Eagle was transferred to the American Protestant Episcopal Church.

When discussing the opening of Alaska, most missionary boards seemed anxious to send their missionaries to this new and fresh field of endeavor, but this was not true of the Episcopal Council of Bishops in 1880. Most of their discussion was pessimistic, revolving around Seward's folly and the foolhardiness of sending a man to a country which was only a jumble of mountains, iceburgs, Indians and Eskimos.

Though the Presbyterian Church had entered the Alaska field in 1877, the Episcopal Board of Missions didn't appoint their first missionary to Alaska until 1886. Mr. Parker was instructed to begin a mission for the Indians somewhere on the Yukon River. He was joined by Mr. Chapman in 1887 and together they established the mission at Anvik, 450 miles up the Yukon River from St. Michael.

It wasn't until 1895 that the General Conference of the Episcopal Church elected a Bishop for Alaska - Peter Trimble Rowe. Bishop Rowe and his wife were Canadians by birth, but had been serving a church in Michigan for fifteen years. He had started his ministry in Canada to an Indian population, giving him a good background for this new position, which many believed was an impossible job.

By January 1896, Bishop Rowe had settled his family in Sitka, which was the capital of Alaska and the only populous district in which to begin his work among the white people. The three existing Episcopal missions at that time were located at Anvik and Fort Adams (near Tanana) on the Yukon River and Point Hope. Bishop Rowe started out in the spring of 1896 to visit and learn about this district to which he had been assigned.

Upon entering the Yukon area, Bishop Rowe found that the missionaries serving under Bishop Wm. C. Bompas (Church of England) had been doing splendid work, traveling down river as far as they found people. The Church of England in Canada and the Episcopal Church in Alaska shared many doctrines and had a good working relationship. The two churches were viewed as interchangeable among the Indians.

As he traveled down river, Bishop Rowe found 600 white residents and 300 Indians at Fortymile. He visited the church's work at Circle City, Fort Yukon and Anvik. At home for the winter, the Bishop had his work cut out for him. He needed to find funds and personnel for boarding schools at Anvik, medical work at Circle City and increase the evangelical outreach from Fort Adams, which soon included Eagle Village.

An annual visit to all the missions, became routine for Bishop Rowe. The next spring he set out over the Chilkoot Pass, accompanied by thousands of gold seekers. They reached Dawson June 4th where they found the city under one to two feet of water and the residents suffering from a serious typhoid epidemic. The Bishop met with Bishop Bompas at Fortymile and discussed the newly surveyed border between Alaska and Canada. The Canadian Church of England missionaries were happy to have their missionary work in Alaska be continued by the Episcopalians.

EAGLE CITY & EAGLE VILLAGE

Just beyond the Canadian border, the Bishop stopped at a new community named Eagle. In 1898, he located two mission lots on twenty-three acres, by setting up corner stakes and then proceeded down river to visit the other churches. When Bishop Rowe returned in 1899, he found that the U.S. Army had used his land as part of their military reservation. The Bishop also found other missionaries established at Eagle, representing the Catholic and Presbyterian Churches. For these reasons, the Bishop confined his work to Eagle Village, rather than establishing a third church in the city.

Mr. Prevost, now stationed at Circle City, included Eagle Village in his evangelical travels. Bishop Rowe always stopped and ministered to the village when he traveled down the Yukon River. Clinics were held for the Eagle Indians and medical care was provided when the Bishop was accompanied by medical personnel headed for their assignments.

In 1904, after the Presbyterians and Catholics closed their churches in Eagle, Bishop Rowe had a chance to purchase to Presbyterian church building for $1,500. He also purchased the improvements (residence) for a total of $3,000. Eagle was gradually developing into the most important towns on the upper Yukon, with a population of 150 soldiers, 250 civilians and about 150 Indians.

Rev. A. R. Hoare served Eagle City in 1905 and 1906. After its purchase, the church was named St. Paul's Mission. The Indians at the Village were also asking for a church, for which they had given a fine site. The Bishop approved the erection of a building for them at the cost of $1500. This was completed during Rev. Hoare's assignment and named St. John's Mission. In 1905, George Boulter, a lay reader and teacher, was assigned to Eagle Village.

During 1905 and 1906, Mr. Boulter held classes in the village church. Twenty-eight students of all ages were enrolled for a five months term. No Indian children had attended the Incorporated School in Eagle City. Though the school was a missionary endeavor, it was supported by the U.S. Department of the Interior, Bureau of Education and was referred to locally as the 'government school.'

In 1907, Rev. Hoare was reassigned to Tanana, and the Bishop appointed Mr. Boulter to include St. Paul's at Eagle City in his duties from 1907 through 1908.

From 1909 through 1920, George B. Burgess served as the missionary to Eagle while the Village teacher was supplied by the Bureau of Education. During the summer of 1909, a new log building was built for the school next to the village church. The property was deeded to the government by the Episcopal Church for one dollar. George Boulter, who had worked in Eagle Village for four years, became the District Superintendent of the Upper Yukon for the Alaska Division of the Bureau of Education.

Though Mr. Burgess started his assignment as a lay reader, he continued his studies while in Eagle and was ordained. His work was very successful at both the white and Indian churches. There was a good attendance at St. Paul's until 1911, when the government Army Post, Fort Egbert, was abandoned.

Mr. Burgess lived in the manse at the St. Paul's Mission in Eagle City. He was very active in community affairs, served on the City Council as the clerk, magistrate and election judge, and was an active participant in both the Arctic Brotherhood. He married his hometown sweetheart in 1911 and their first child, a son, was born October 11, 1915. While Rev. Burgess was out on a year's furlough in 1914, "Big Jim" kept up the services and cared for the spiritual needs of the villagers. In 1918 Mrs. Burgess and her son visited relatives in Tennessee and in August 1919, Mr. Burgess joined his wife, leaving his Eagle assignment permanently.

Mr. Burgess Gaither, a relative of Mr. Burgess, served as a temporary substitute to the Eagle area, and later received a permanent assignment. Mr. Gaither had just been discharged from the Army following World War I. He was a lay-reader preparing for Holy Orders and served Eagle for five years from 1920 through 1925. He also served as the government teacher at the Village during those years. Mr. Gaither wrote elegantly about the grandeur of the country, loving it more every passing day.

Mr. Gaither was concerned about the condition of the village. The site for a new village had been laid out long before, but only five new cabins had been built. "The entire population needs to change abode and for the sake of health, the old cabins should be razed and burned. This is the only sane, and sensible course, for the native is a camper by nature and some of them will not be made into housekeepers."

Mr. Gaither left Eagle in 1925. For the next two years there was no resident Missionary, but visits were made by Bishop Rowe and Archdeacon Drane with the assistance of an Indian Lay-reader, Walter Benjamin, who was appointed to assist in conducting the services at the Indian Village. Bishop Rowe transferred the Rev. G. H. Moody from Fort Yukon to Eagle in 1926 where he worked for three years, assisted by Walter Benjamin at the Village. Little is known about his work, except that he retired in August 1929 and moved to the lower states. Rev. and Mrs. Arthur G. Fullerton, formerly stationed at Tanana, were appointed to fill the vacancy. The Fullertons noted that the Indians seemed to have had better instruction and more advantages in their school, for when asked about an interpreter, the majority of the villagers wished the services in English, without an interpreter.

Rev. A. G. and Mrs. Fullerton lived in St. Paul's manse from 1930-1947 and also served the Indian Village with the able assistance of Walter Ben. The Fullertons were a dedicated lay couple, with a strong background in the Episcopal Church. Mrs. Fullerton was a sister to Bishop Rowe's second wife. Each season the Fullertons received a fine supply of clothing from the supporting Woman's Auxiliaries. The Indian women were anxious to bring their bed work, moccasins and dried fish to trade for the clothing.

SARAH AND WALTER BENJAMIN
Courtesy: Eagle Historical Society

VILLAGE CONGREGATION WITH WALTER BENJAMIN
Courtesy: Eagle Historical Society

In the August 1936 issue of The Alaskan Churchman, Mr. Fullerton began a campaign to seek donations to erect a large white cross on top of the high Eagle Bluff. He thought the cross would serve as a Memorial to remind the people of Bishop Rowe's first voyage down the Yukon and to mark the spot where he first entered the interior of his vast diocese. During the summer of 1938, they were ready to erect the cross, which was already constructed. When they climbed to the summit of the Bluff, they found that the ridge was so narrow it prevented the men from working on it safety and the rock on the north face of the cliff was badly disintegrated, so they decided to erect the cross on the high bank of the river, on the mission property, overlooking the Yukon. The cross was painted with durable aluminum paint, and was plainly visible for a long distance on the river.

The large cross was not the only building endeavor completed by the Fullertons. In 1936-37, a large two story rectory was built to replace the single story one they had purchased from the Presbyterians. This new log residence was very modern, compared to the other Eagle residences. The first floor contained a kitchen, pantry, study and large living room for social activities. There were three bedrooms and a bathroom upstairs. There was a full basement which contained a cistern to catch the rain water and a hot water tank next to the large furnace which furnished hot water to the kitchen and the modern bathroom on the second floor. There was a tunnel between the house and the church which contained pipes attached to the furnace to provide heat in the church. The Fullertons were outstanding gardeners, not only providing many of their vegetables but the large front yard of the church and residence was full of beautiful flowers.

In 1938 the Fullertons returned from their furlough with their usual energy. Rev. Fullerton had long dreamed of replacing the original church which was still in use. To obtain the necessary materials, he purchased the remains of the Fort Egbert hospital. With the help of Horace Biederman, the old church was razed and rebuilt in 1943 and 1944. The Fullertons retired in June 1946, after seventeen years at Eagle and one year at Tanana. They left a splendid new church and rectory, both monuments to their vision, industry and determination.

In the fall of 1946, Laurence A. Crossen and his daughter Grace arrived at Eagle to serve as lay readers from the Diocese of Long Island. Walter Benjamin continued to assist the Crossens as a lay reader at the Village, work he had been doing for more than thirty years. Mr. Crossen held services in both churches, walking to the village in all kinds of weather for the service. Miss Crosson was a nurse and took care of the health of both communities. Most every day there was a clinic in her kitchen.

Mr. Crosson and his daughter were both appreciated by the Eagle communities. However, there continued to be a shortage of church personnel. Early in 1949, there was a critical shortage of nurses at the Hudson Stuck Memorial Hospital at Fort Yukon and because of the increase in patients, Miss Crosson had to be temporarily transferred to relieve the need there. Walter Benjamin, lay reader at Eagle Village, died in August 1951. Mr. Crosson retired the same year.

After this year, Eagle was only served intermittently by resident church workers. The Episcopal Bishops visited the Eagle area as often as possible and held services and ministered the sacraments of the Church. Bishop Rowe died in 1942 at the age of eighty-six; John Bentley served as Bishop of the Missionary District of Alaska until he resigned in 1947 to accept election as Vice-President of the National Council and Director of the Overseas Department.

Deacon William J. Gordon, Jr. served briefly in Seward in 1943 before being advanced to the priesthood. He was then sent to the St. Thomas Mission at Point Hope. After Bishop Bentley's resignation, Rev. Gordon was elected the third Missionary Bishop of Alaska in 1947. However he had to wait until 1948 to reach the canonical age of thirty in order to be consecrated. The next year Bishop Gordon learned to fly to save the expense of hiring commercial planes and to help unify the forty centers of Episcopal faith in Alaska, thus earning the nick-name "The Flying Bishop."

Rev. Norman Elliott spent a year at Eagle from 1953-54. He returned later for six months during the winter of 1958 when he also taught school in the Indian village. The church leased the village school building from the Village Council for Rev. Elliott's use. Another resident priest to serve in Eagle was Rev. Richard Treadwell, who was stationed in Eagle for one year, from 1965 to 1966.

In 1968, a youth group and their sponsors from the church in Anchorage came to Eagle to work on the church buildings. For the manse, they built a new rock foundation, replaced rotten base logs, installed new tile on the kitchen floor and leveled the building as much as possible which required rehanging all the windows and doors. They also replaced rotten basement walls under the church and between the house and the church and installed a new floor in the church basement. Stone steps were constructed at the church and mission house and rain gutters were installed. While the outside work was going on, the ladies washed all of the walls and windows, painted the kitchen walls, and the living room walls, doors and floor. New drapes were made for the living room. The group cut and stockpiled fire wood on the back porch.

One of Bishop Gordon's greatest challenges was trying to find workers for all of the position in the churches. He assigned seminary students four different summers to Eagle; each brought different talents. They wrote elegant articles describing the Eagle area, the people and their summer activities. What an education they must have received, writing and preaching and working with their parishioners. These young men planned many activities and outings for the children, and at the end of the summer there several young people were confirmed. The Flying Bishop tried to make at least an annual visit to Eagle to hold services, administer the sacraments and bring food for a picnic. Everyone looked forward to his visits. Later the Fairbanks Priest came to Eagle irregularly and held services. The Church leaders continually challenged both the city and village to find lay leaders within their communities to hold services regularly.

Parishioners in both communities continued to plead for a full time minister, but this seemed to be an impossibility. Following Rev. Treadwell's year of residency in 1965, the members of St. Paul's held weekly meetings with local residents leading the service. Apparently this was not completely satisfactory, as in 1967 they obtained a missionary couple, Donna & Max Embree, from the Central Alaska Mission Headquarters in Glennallen, who came and lived in Eagle. This arrangement has continued to the present time with the local group becoming an autonomous group, called the Eagle Bible Chapel. Local residents provide some leadership and assist the missionary. The Episcopalians gave permission for individual missionaries to use the Eagle Church facilities. Their only request was that they not attempt to tear down the theological thinking of the people who were traditionally members of the Episcopal Church. When a Catholic Priest visits Eagle, his services are also held in the St. Paul's Mission. December 23, 1996 with the temperature -35 degrees F., the parsonage burned to the ground. The fire had started with a chimney fire, as the building was being heated for a service. Though the parsonage and the church were attached with a wooden hallway, Eagle's volunteer fire department was able to save the church building by cutting the hallway down.

The parishioners at Eagle Village strongly felt the absence of a resident minister. They have never given up trying to find someone to visit the village at regular intervals. In 1976 John and Sandy FourBear, lay leaders from the Sioux Tribe in South Dakota, moved to Eagle to minister to the residents. They lived in the St. Paul's manse and held services in the village. The Indians loved visiting with them in town, but after two years, the FourBears were transferred to Arctic Village. Besides the Episcopal Bishop and Priests, the villagers have been able to persuade Church of England Priests from Dawson to visit the village and hold services. Some of them have tried to visit monthly, but there have been long periods without any services. There continues to be a strong tie between the Indians living in Dawson and Eagle; these are the only two remaining villages of the Han Indians and many of them are related.

THE WHITE CROSS

The large white wooden cross had remained in the church yard on the river bank for many years. Each time Bishop Bentley visited Eagle, he told the young ministers, if they ran out of work they could take that cross and put it up on the bluff where it belonged. In 1958, Bill Baldrich, one of the summer seminary students assigned to Eagle, asked Anton Merly if he thought they could get that cross up on the bluff to its original intended site. Anton was an ingenious hard worker and he agreed to assist with the project. They floated the parts down the river to the base of the bluff. Many from Eagle Village and Tanacross offered to help, but it ended up with just Anton, Bill and Bob Stacey. The larger piece of wood was 20 feet long and was a 10"x10" Douglas fir timber. After several unsuccessful trials, they finally figured out how to wench the two pieces up the hill. Two men cranked the wench and Anton kept the rollers under the timber. After getting the large timber in place, Anton made a rope ladder to fasten the cross piece on. They sanded and painted it, taking a total of seven days to complete the project. Bill helped to the end, even though he was afraid of heights and had to crawl up the hill; he never would look up at the cross while Anton was on it.

The cross stayed in place until the fall of 1966 when the base rotted off and the wind blew it over. The cross was on a mining claim at the time. Fred Jenkins had the claim and said if he had been in town, he wouldn't have let them put the cross up. But he

136

FULLERTONS AND CROSS ON RIVER BANK
Courtesy: Eagle Historical Society

he was in town in 1966 when the cross blew down. When he heard that
Anton planned to repair the cross, he walked back and forth in
front of Anton's house for three days with his .45 pistol strapped
to his waist, saying "nobody is going to walk on my claims again."
So the cross was never put up again and the remains rest on the
ground by the present flag pole which is on the bluff.

CHAPTER 10

SOCIAL ORGANIZATIONS

Eagle City was a very social community; the only entertainment available was of local origin. The first church sponsored weekly song fests and the military invited everyone to their activities - dances, baseball and basketball games, bowling, etc.

Some of the residents were members of the Yukon Order of Pioneers, which had been organized at the town of Fortymile in 1893. The membership requirement was residency in the watershed of the Yukon and it's tributaries from 1893-1896, thus making it impossible for most of Eagle's residents to become members. Then the Arctic Brotherhood (AB) was organized in 1899. When some of the AB members moved to Nome, they were not permitted to form an AB chapter as they did not meet the requirement of living within the Yukon River watershed. In frustration, they started a new organization in Nome in 1907 which they called Pioneers of Alaska; the Grand Igloo was organized in 1908. Their membership requirement was residence in any part of Alaska before December 31, 1900. The Women's Auxiliary organized in 1911 for the wives, mothers and sister of Pioneers and all women residing in Alaska prior to December 31, 1900.

Some local residents retained their membership in the Masonic Lodge which reported holding annual banquets on St. John's Day (December). In 1902 it was held in the Courtroom.

The Haymakers Association was organized in Eagle in 1907. Their special terminology included the hay loft (lodge building), bundles (dollars) and straws (cents). They rented the Redmen Lodge for seven dollars a night where they sponsored many socials. The Dancing Club transferred their money to the Haymakers and joined them when they promised to sponsor at least two dances a month.

The only two organizations which had their own lodge buildings and lasted for any length of time in Eagle were the Improved Order of Red Men and the Arctic Brotherhood. Their major differences were that the Arctic Brotherhood was an International Fraternity which placed their emphasis on the north and gold mining and permitted the use of alcohol during their social events. The Improved Order of Redmen was a purely patriotic American Fraternity and did not allow the use of alcohol in their wigwam nor bartenders or gamblers to be members.

IMPROVED ORDER OF RED MEN

The Improved Order of Red Men is one of the oldest organizations of its type in America, having been organized in 1765 under the name of Sons of Liberty. They were part of the group who met in Boston in 1773 to protest the tax on tea imposed by England. When their protest went unheeded, they disguised themselves as Mohawk Indians, proceeded to Boston harbor and dumped overboard 342 chests of English tea.

After the American Revolution the name was changed to The Order of Red Men. They kept the customs and terminology of the Indians as a basic part of the Fraternity. The Order of Red Men is a non-profit patriotic Fraternity chartered by Congress, devoted to inspiring a greater love for the United States of America and the principles of American Liberty.

The motto of the organization is Freedom, Friendship, Charity and their goals are three fold:
     To teach and exemplify the principles of friendship and brotherly helpfulness.
     To extend the brotherhood of man through fraternal love and good fellowship.
     To be acknowledged as conservators of the history, the customs and the virtues of the original American people.

Each tribe was required to be named after some Indian tribe or chief connected with the locality where it was instituted. Each is intended to teach a lesson which illustrated Indian life and Indian characteristics. A ladies auxiliary was named Degree of Pocohantas and a juvenile group was formed in 1915 for boys and girls in separate branches.

CHETUTHUTLIE TRIBE NO. 6
HUNTING GROUNDS: EAGLE
RESERVATION: ALASKA

The first regular Council meeting was held in Eagle on June 16, 1904 in the Arctic Brotherhood Hall, becoming the farthest north tribe. At this meeting eighteen charter members were admitted.
The name of the Eagle tribe, Chetuthutlie, was selected which literally means 'The rock that turns the water', after the Eagle Bluff which juts into the Yukon River. A log lodge building was completed and dedicated on New Year's Eve 1904.

The early population of Eagle, the hunting grounds, was a floating one with many members leaving Eagle. The largest number of members was in 1909 when there were 103 brothers. In 1918 there were 46 members, even though the total male population of the city was 50.

Meetings were held weekly on Thursday evening. They often included

OFFICERS OF THE IMPROVED ORDER OF REDMEN
Courtesy: Eagle Historical Society

card games, a lunch and the brothers telling stories of their varied, interesting experiences in the far north. Every second week at the conclusion of their lodge meeting, they entertained all who cared to join them, usually having a dance on those nights. In 1908, the Order purchased a large pump organ to provide music for their functions. As a secret fraternity, the windows were covered with shutters during the meeting. To be admitted to the meeting, one rang a doorbell and was admitted after being identified through the peep hole in the door.

The IOORM had excellent sick and burial benefits. These were very important for the bachelors living far from their families. Widows often wrote to request the benefits. For these reasons, many members retained their membership in the Eagle order, after moving from the area.

MEMBERS OF THE IMPROVED ORDER OF REDMEN
Courtesy: Eagle Historical Society

By the 1940's, IOORM membership had dropped to 13 and officers had
to serve in two positions. The last meeting was held July 3, 1941.
In 1944 Wyman Fritsch wrote that the Improved Order of Red Men was
defunct due to a lack of members, though he continued to submit
annual reports until 1950. The property was later sold to Wyman.
In 1993, Wyman's heirs donated the property to the Eagle Historical
Society who cleaned it up and have worked to restore the 30' x 60'
building to be used for community functions, the society office and
work room.

The fraternal organization, Arctic Brotherhood, began as a joke aboard the steamer "City of Seattle" headed for Skagway in February 1899. A group of returning "sourdoughs", who had already been over the gold rush trails and knew their hardships, offered to initiate the "cheechakos" aboard into those hardships. They improvised a strenuous ceremony into the Arctic Brotherhood. The participants decided that such an order was just exactly what was needed in that new country. A council was held, a ritual, by-laws and constitution were adopted and Camp Skagway No. 1 was duly organized and was called the Mother Camp thereafter. Few changes were ever made in the original documents. (Davidson, pg. 8)

The Preamble of the Constitution stated, "The object of this organization shall be to encourage and promote social and intellectual intercourse and benevolence among its members, and to advance the interests of its members, and those of the Northwest section of North America." The area encompassed all of Alaska, the Yukon Territory, all of the Northwest Territory and British Columbia, north of parallel 54 degrees, 20 minutes, north latitude. This area was strictly adhered to and no subordinate camp was permitted south of the designated line. Membership was open to any male person over 16 years and six months of age, and of good moral character.

Over the organizations symbol of a gold pan with U.S. and British flags was written "No boundary line here." This was in reference to the differences existing between the subjects of Uncle Sam and those of the British Empire, concerning the dispute then being carried on over the true boundary line dividing these two governments.

By 1909 the Arctic Brotherhood was organized into 24 Camps in every important section of the North, on both the American and Canadian sides of the border. Though it was not a political organization, the order made itself felt in both Washington and Ottawa and influenced legislation in behalf of Alaska and the Yukon Territory. The Arctic Brotherhood sponsored an Alaska-Yukon-Pacific Exposition in 1910 at Seattle.

CAMP EAGLE NO. 13

Camp Eagle of the Arctic Brotherhood was organized in May 1901. In 1903 a large frame lodge building was construct which was located on three city lots on the corner of Berry & 3rd Street, which was at the entrance into Fort Egbert. There were between 60 and 70 members in good standing on the roll in 1904. In 1907, a large gold pan was placed on the front of the building.

Social events were sponsored immediately. These often included "Smokers" held in November on election nights, music for the basket

socials, masquerade dances on Valentine's Day, entertainment for
St. Patricks Day which was usually a dance and the Christmas eve.
celebration which included a Christmas tree, dance and
entertainment.

PERFORMANCE IN ARCTIC BROTHERHOOD LODGE
Courtesy: Eagle Historical Society

Special events were also sponsored. In 1908 a special dance was
given in honor of Dr. Schmitter, the military doctor at Fort Egbert
who was being transferred. In 1913, the town arranged a special
benefit dance for Abe Malm to raise money to assist with his
medical and travel expenses to Seattle.

Lighting of the hall with just kerosene lamps was a problem. In
April 1917, it was voted to purchase a gasoline lighting system. In
October an ingenious carbide light plant was installed.

October 7, 1921, the meeting of the Arctic Brotherhood Camp Eagle
No. 13 was called by the Arctic Chief Tom King. There was a long

discussion upon the status and the future of the organization. It was voted to disband and appoint three caretakers to look after the property. The twelve members in good standing designated themselves as THE EAGLE CLUB.

In 1925, Wm. Fritsch became the owner of Lots 7, 8, and 9 in Block 5 two of which he had been gardening. Eventually the AB Lodge building was torn down.

                            CHAPTER 11

                            HAN INDIANS

The first arrivals in North America were groups of nomadic hunters
traveling from Asia over a land bridge known as Beringia. Recent
archaeological evidence suggests the first migrations may have
occurred as long ago as 40,000 years. Successive waves of people
moved across the land bridge, which appeared and disappeared as the
earth's temperatures changed over time, creating Ice Ages flooding
the land during warm periods. Slowly, the new inhabitants spread
across the continent, arriving at the southern tip of South America
some 10,000 years ago. (Crowe, 1974:2)

One such migrant group were the Athabascan Indians, of which the
Han Indians are a sub-group. The Han occupied the upper Yukon area
between the Charley River, Alaska and Nuklako, Yukon Territory.
Small family groups lived in tents of caribou skin covering a
willow frame. Several households formed a local group and a number
of local groups constituted a band, which occupied a well defined
territory. The Han Indians had four major bands and later villages
were established at Charley River, Johnny's Village (at Eagle),
Fortymile and Nuklako (across the river from Fort Reliance in the
Yukon Territory, Canada).

Originally the Han Indians migrated during the year to their
sources of food. Summers were spent on the rivers fishing, drying
their catch, tanning moose and caribou skins from animals killed
during the winter hunt, hunting and drying game and picking
berries. In September they moved inland to construct and repair
caribou corrals, into which they drove the animals during the
caribou's fall migration. Most game caught during the fall hunt was
cached for winter use. In Mid-October, after the brief hunt, the
Han returned to the river camps, spending the next few months
sewing winter clothing, hunting in the area, and bringing in meat
from the caches to feed the people. Usually by January, the people
returned inland for the winter caribou hunt, which lasted until
March, when preparation for the fishing season began once again
(Dawson, 1988:5).

The Han used dogs mainly to carry backpacks or to pull a travois
loaded with their skin tents and supplies. They used caribou and
moose hides to make their clothing and boots, as well as their
shelters. Shell-bead money was used and people were interested in
collecting furs and food, but were not preoccupied with wealth or
status.

Animals played an important role in Han culture. The Han would not
eat dog, wolf, raven, hawk or eagle. The bear had a special meaning
for them. Many of their legends speak of the bear as a man. The
otter was regarded as a bad luck symbol. Wolverine, a cousin to
man, was seldom eaten (Schmitter, 1985:1-20).

The Spartan toughening of Athabascans was an essential part of their ancient training for adulthood and their daily lives. From the time a boy was turned over to his maternal uncle at about the age of six, he was subjected to every hardship of cold and forced labor with the view to an ultimate development of physical strength and the powers of endurance. This undoubtedly accounted for the once successful adaptation of the interior Indian to his environment of snow and severe cold, with clothing and housing which were flimsy compared to that of the Eskimos.

Even before white men entered the upper Yukon area, the natives were trading with the coastal Indians and lower Yukon River Indians, obtaining Russian beads, guns, traps and kettles. They reported having serious epidemics during that time, including symptoms of tuberculosis. It was a hard life and starvation continued to be a common event.

The Indians at Eagle Village talk of the times when family groups used to live in skin houses up Mission Creek in the winter before the white men arrived. There water, caribou meat and wood were available and being in the woods they were protected from the wind. One winter while there, a smallpox epidemic wiped out most of them. Some of the dead were buried in hollow logs on the bluff by the river.

Expansion of the fur trade brought the Han Indians into the first contact with white men in their area. The first recorded white man to travel down the Upper portion of the Yukon River through the Han territory was Robert Campbell, Chief Trader for the Hudson Bay Company in 1851. (Campbell, 1851:96-97). Finding the Indians in large bands in camps, he noted they were very friendly and astonished at seeing visitors, because they had never seen either a white man or one of his boats before.

In 1880, Francois Mercier built a trading post at Eagle near the present boat landing (Mercier 1986:2 and 32). He called the single log house trading post "Belleisle", after a friend living in San Francisco. Finding little business there, Mercier left this post in search of areas with more furs, though he returned and opened the post several times between 1882 and 1896. Remains of Indian house pits are clustered together in this same area, at which archeological excavations have been done and the artifacts are on exhibit in the Eagle Museum. The Indians later built a village farther up the river, near the present Indian graveyard where there is more sunshine during the winter.

Lieutenant Schwatka, on a U. S. Army reconnaissance trip down the Yukon River in 1883, stopped at the Eagle Village for several days (Schwatka 1893:251). He noted that Eagle had the first Indian village they had encountered on the river which deserved to be referred to as permanent. Even there, the logs of which the six cabins were built, seemed to be mere poles. The body of the houses

were of a very inferior construction, in which ventilation seemed
to be the predominate idea. The large door in front was roughly

INDIAN CAMP AT EAGLE
Courtesy: Eagle Historical Society

closed by a well-riddled moose or caribou skin. The roofs were of
skins battened down by spruce poles, which projected beyond the
walls in irregular lengths, often six or eight feet, giving the
whole village a most bristly appearance. A fire was built on the
dirt floor in the center of the room, and the smoke was left to get
out the best way it could. As the occupants were generally sitting
flat on the floor, or stretched out at full length on their backs
or stomachs in the dirt, they were in a stratum of air
comparatively clear, or at least, endurable to Indian lungs. The
ascending smoke found ample air-holes among the upper cracks of the
walls, while the dense mass of it which was retained under the
skins of the roof, making it almost impossible to stand upright,
was utilized for smoking the salmon which were hung up in this
space. Schwatka noted that it appeared to be an old village built
close to the eroding river bank. The Indian name of the village was
Klat-ol-klin, but it was generally known as Johnny's Village, after
the Chief's americanized name.

Schwatka also found the traders site about a mile or a mile and a
quarter below Klat-ol-klin and on the same side of the river.
Although the Indians obtained a few white man's manufactured items
from the earlier traders, their life style was not materially

147

changed until the 1896 gold rush brought hordes of miners into their area. Mission activity among the Han Indians was closely correlated with the gold rush. Hudson Stuck, the Episcopal priest, always felt that the Klondike gold rush of 1897 and 1898 brought nothing but harm to the native people of Alaska. At least it brought a regular food supply so there were fewer periods of starvation for the Indians.

The Indians were curious about these new arrivals in their country and were helpful to them in many ways. When the United States Army was sent to Alaska in 1898 to build roads and trails overland into the Interior of Alaska, the Indian guided them over their trails. However, the Indian guides refused to travel beyond their own territory, as the law of trespassing on the territory of other tribes was rigidly enforced, the penalty being the death of the invader if caught, unless they showed a permit from the Chief of the country they were traveling through. (Rice 1900:784).

The Indian communities were suddenly saturated with large numbers of new contacts which brought a rapid social change to the native groups. Tuberculosis became a scourge for the natives; it was present in all its forms and stages. The tuberculosis bacillus was given full credit for their devastation for many years. It is now felt that the social disruption or rapid social change was a greater factor in changing the native culture than were unsanitary conditions, crowding, and poverty.

Later, the site of Johnny's village was moved farther up river to the present location. After Eagle City was established in 1897, the village was called Eagle Village. In 1910, the population of the native village was estimated to be 200.

ELIZA MALCOLM

- 1982

On August 18, 1982, Eagle's oldest resident, Eliza Malcolm, died at her home in the village. Her funeral was held on August 20th with Andy Fairfield, an Episcopal minister, officiating. She was buried in the Eagle Village cemetery. Her exact age was unknown, but was estimated to be between 100 and 120 years. When Eliza was born, "Family don't write birthdays, don't know how to write," her sister-in-law, Sarah Malcolm, explained. Eliza had been baptized in 1896 when she was a teenager.

Eliza's father was Chief Robert and her mother was Susan. The family lived at LaPierre House on the Bell River in the Yukon Territory, Canada where Eliza was born. Her father worked for the Hudson Bay Company and was the proud owner of an old flintlock rifle. Eliza had lots of brothers and sisters. One sister married a minister and lived at Mayo, Y.T. Even though she was blind in her old age, she and Eliza visited back and forth each summer as long as they could.

Sarah Malcolm remembered Eliza telling stories about her life when she was young, and said "she would cry when she talked about old days. Her family migrated around the Peel and Porcupine Rivers, hunting, trapping and fishing about 100 miles from Fort McPherson. They lived in skin houses. The dogs carried the housepoles like a travois; men and women also carried poles. Her mom made big birch bark baskets, folding four corners and sewing willow around the edges with roots, making large stitches. She used the baskets to store berries and fish eggs, also to hold water. Talk about lots of blueberries, cranberries and salmon berries. Always lots of fun picking berries. They tanned lots of winter hides each spring, camping by a creek. They had grayling then, making their own fish hooks. Had lots of meat soup with rice.

"When young, her Mom and Dad say, 'Eliza do this, Eliza do that,' and she had to go out - no gun, take bow and arrows. She was left handed, but she brought home rabbits and ptarmigans. One time feathers really fly, but so did the bird. Another time she brought home fourteen ground squirrels, carrying them in a caribou skin bag with moosehide straps. She put dry moss in the bag after gutting the squirrels, so the bag would not get wet. She would hang them over the campfire and smoke them or boil with a little rice. They used the squirrel skins for babies clothes. The adults wore caribou skin clothes, which the women made from hides they had tanned. Dresses had long sleeves and were tight around the neck to protect from mosquitos, not much fringe. Women that worked, not lazy, decorated dresses with quill work. They made gloves for the men with long cuffs to protect their arms from mosquitos."

Eliza married a young man, Benjamin. They also migrated around the

149

country and raised a large family. She remembered that first husband as one who was never mad at her. They trapped and snared ground squirrels and made fish net for graying. There were not many porcupines, but they did get caribou. They went to Rampart House where they caught white fish. They also traded there with Mr. Firth who had a large store and spoke their native language. They also traded at Fort McPherson and Dawson, taking down two, three or four loads of furs, trading them for ammunition, tea, sugar, flour and baking powder and rice.

After Eliza's first husband died, she traveled to Eagle with a group of Indians. There she met her second husband, Joe Malcolm and they raised another family. In all, Eliza had eleven children. Sarah Malcolm and Eliza were sister-in-laws and the two families traveled and trapped together. Eliza used to help younger Sarah and tell her, "Don't be scared night time, keep fire going." They used tents when out on the trap line and had the tents face each other with a fire in between. They had small Yukon wood stoves inside the tents and spruce bough beds with caribou skin mattresses. The women worked outside whenever possible, only moving inside the tent to work when it rained. Both families traveled with small children. Eliza was very strong and always worked hard. Sarah said, "She work all the time like a man. When 50 degrees below zero, she would take tent down and move, taking little children."

Eliza and Joe Malcolm remained in Eagle Village during their later years. Eliza enjoyed having her people from Peel River visit. She would always fix a big dinner for her family.

Joe Malcolm died from cancer on May 11, 1972 at the Fairbanks Hospital. After that, Eliza's youngest daughter, Louise Paul, and her family cared for Eliza at Eagle. Eliza liked to attend church, walk about the village and carry in a stick or two of wood each day. She never learned to speak English, but always enjoyed having visitors, talking to them in her native tongue. Always wearing a smile, she earned the nickname 'Happy'. One time she had pneumonia and was sent into the Fairbanks Hospital. After that experience, she asked her family never to send her to the hospital again, as "they hurt me." Eliza died at home, with her family gathered around her, giving all of them instructions on the day of her death and telling them she would be leaving them. She was ready.

Eliza's Eagle friends all considered it a great privilege to have known this grand old matriarch. What an excellent role model she provided, in coping with such great changes within her long life span. As she instructed on her death bed, "Life goes on. Take care of each other and don't cry."

SARAH MALCOLM

1905-1991

Sarah Malcolm was a delightful Indian lady who lived at Eagle
Village. She loved to get together with the ladies in Eagle City
and talk about her life, while she beaded or made birch bark
baskets. She was always busy with her crafts, for which there was
a ready market. She eagerly taught these crafts to her friends. She
lived a full and rich life.

Sarah's Dad, Steven Simon, was born in Eagle; her Mom, Phoebe, was
from Fort McPhearson. She had come to Eagle with a group of her
people one spring where she met Big Steve. After they were married,
she never returned to Fort McPhearson, even for a visit.

The McPhearson residents came to Eagle frequently when they had a
lot of furs to trade or lots of moose and caribou hides to sell, so
they could buy ammunition, tea and rice or whatever they needed.
Some of the Eagle men used to go to Canada to trap, but they had to
go to Dawson to sell their furs.

FAMILY

Sarah was born in Eagle in 1905. She had two brothers, but they
both died young. Her memories of childhood were of spending winters
in a tent on the Seventymile River or Sheep Creek, while her Dad
hunted for moose or trapped for lynx, mink and marten. They used
lots of snares. Her Dad put up a cache for the meat and built a
tent frame with high walls and a home made door. The teacher sent
paper, pencil and books with them and Sarah used to write. When her
Dad wasn't doing much trapping, he cut wood for the steamboats at
Sheep Creek. At the same time, he hunted and killed moose and lots
of caribou, earning the name "Caribou Steve." He gave away a lot of
meat. When Sarah stayed with a family at the village to work, her
Dad would give them a whole moose.

During the summer, Steve and Phoebe went down to Shade Creek to
fish for King Salmon, which they dried for the winter. They stayed
about a month, making their own dip nets out of twine from the
trading store. Babiche was used before they learned to use the
thirteen ply twine. They traded dried salmon at the Mission for
good clothes.

CHILDHOOD

Games were played at the old village school. They didn't have a
dance hall, so the teacher let them use the school house during
their one week Christmas holiday. They took out all the seats
through the window, providing lots of room. They had two gas lamps
with the teacher providing them the gas. They had a whole week to
dance.

Sarah was still small, but she liked to stand on the benches and watch the square dancing. Violins provided the music, not guitars. Big Jim Juneby, the village Marshal, played the violin. The teacher told them to go ahead and dance. Some of the white people showed the Indians how to dance and Sarah learned to square dance. Some learned to do the Red River Jig from the Peel River Indians when they visited Eagle; they did that dance at Fort McPhearson and at Rampart House. Martha Malcolm and Louise Paul used to dance a good jig.

After the dance, they used to play native games. They would cut around and around a white caribou skin, ending with a long rope. They would stretch the rope out around the room and people would sit down on the floor along the rope or kneel on one knee. One man would put a ring on the rope and they would pass it along the rope. One person had to find the ring. When they found the person with the ring, he had to get up and dance. The people would sing an Indian song first and then make the person dance; some of the people didn't like it. Sometimes the men were too lazy to get up, and everyone laughed and made them get up and dance and the children all laughed. Then that man had to start to look for the ring. Only the women and men played the game, with the children watching.

They had a native chief who used to work with the teacher. The two would talk about ways to treat the village and the teacher did what the chief said. The chief used to make speeches. The warriors danced, coming in all dressed up and sang for the people. There were lots of people at the village then and there were big crowds at the dances singing. Sarah didn't remember any of the songs, but there were all kinds of different native songs from Dawson, about the Stick Indians, old men and old people.

More recently, Louise Paul, Harry David, Hannah Stevens, Willie Juneby and even Totsie's grandmother, used to teach the kids how to dance the old Indian dances. They put on Indian clothes, wore feathers and looked like real natives, dancing to celebrate the New Year. Sarah wished they would still dance like that at Eagle Village. At Tanana Crossing and Dot Lake, they continued the dances, but at Eagle, they just let it go.

They used to play other games that took all day. They used to hide something and others had to look for it. Sometimes it was a good knife, and whoever found it, got to keep it. They used to hide lots of good things. Sometimes they pounded dry meat and put some bone grease with it, put it in clean moose or caribou skin and hide it. They played this game anytime of the year, but mostly in the summer.

They used to make toys for the children, making them out of cottonwood bark, cutting with a snowshoe knife. They made little boats, lots of little snowshoes, Indian dolls with a piece of caribou skin with braided black silk hair. Sarah liked to play with dolls. They also liked to embroider, which they had learned to do in school.

While at the trapping camp, Sarah's mother taught her to cut meat. She didn't want it to spoil, so she cut the meat thin and dried it, sometimes putting on a little salt for drying.

During the summer time, they moved back to the village before the mosquitos arrived. They set up three to five tents, clearing all the brush around the tents, put a scarf over the door and built a big smokey fire in the clearing. There was no school during the summer and Sarah stayed with a lady who taught her to tan moose and caribou hides when she was ten years old. Sarah's Dad would give her something, like a beaver hide for teaching Sarah. Their source of water was a spring behind the village school. The Yukon River water was too muddy.

Later on Sarah's Dad told her she should stay home during the winter to go to school. She remembers that at the first school, the students didn't know anything; it was hard for them. Then the preacher took them to Sunday School where they learned to count with blocks and colored sticks. There were just a few small children in school. Next time the preacher brought a slate and pencil so they could write their names. They couldn't write like the preacher and some of the kids cried. When the preacher came back again, there was a blackboard and chalk. The kids that were ready to write, used that. Pretty soon they could write their names. Sarah went to school through the 8th grade and went to Sunday School all of the time.

MARRIAGE

In 1920, Sarah married Edward Malcolm, who was from Fort Olgivie, Canada. They had eleven children, eight boys and three girls. Sarah's mother, Phoebe, died of tuberculosis the year Sarah's first baby was born.

After Ed Malcolm's brother, Joe, came to Eagle and married Eliza, the two families used to go trapping together at Sheep Creek. In the summer time they went there to hunt moose, packing the dogs. They blazed their trail on the trees with axes. After they got a moose, they would dry the meat to make it lighter and pack it home on the dogs. They would stay out for three weeks, working hard. They took a little warm tent and had lots of good caribou skin mattresses to sleep on. Sarah would pack the babies.

One summer, Sarah and Eliza were camping out together when a caribou herd came near their camp. They were worried because they didn't know where their kids had gone, but the children came back with one fat bull caribou. They also returned with a lot of

153

SARAH MALCOLM 1991
Courtesy: Cassalona D'Alessandro

ptarmigan eggs in their hats. When Sarah asked where they got the
still warm eggs, the boys said the chickens (grouse or spruce hen)
laid the eggs, all twelve of them. Sarah put grease in the frying
pan and when she broke the eggs in it, they sounded just like
chicken eggs cooking.

They returned to Eagle after the fall hunt. They built a big strong
cache for their meat, putting tin around the bottom of the cache
legs so they wouldn't crack or get rotten and to prevent small
animals from entering. They made a good ladder of logs. When it was
all finished, they put a big padlock on the door with a big chain.
They put lots of stuff in the cache and it kept like new.

Late in the fall the families went out to trap, walking with their
dogs packed. They returned home for Christmas with dog teams. Sarah
drove one team and her husband drove another team. After Christmas
they returned to their trapping grounds. The weather was cold,
often 50 or 60 degrees below zero. They all had warm clothes; Eliza
helped Sarah make some of them. Sarah wore a big size bib overall,
good men's underwear and a parka. Alexia used to make fur boots for
her. They put ground squirrel skins around their sleeves, like a
lining, making it real warm. Eliza used to snare the squirrels and
tan the hides.

While the families were out on the trap line, they lived in tents
during the cold weather. The men would put up two tents with a wood
stove and cut lots of firewood by the tent. The tents would be
thirty feet apart; if they were to close to each other, it was not
good for the dogs. The yards were clean with a place for the kids
to play. They burned lots and lots of candles out on the trap line.
Sometimes they built a big campfire outside between the tents.
Eliza taught Sarah how to cook meat and dried potatoes over a
campfire. She told her when you cook indoors, you use lots and lots
of wood to keep up the fire, so she had better learn to cook
outdoors. But they fried meat on the stove inside and boiled water
to make tea. They had lots of good meat out on the trap line -
caribou, sheep and moose. They had to cover up the meat with a big
canvas to protect it from the winged camp robbers. They used to
make shortening in five gallon cans.

When they went home in the spring, they used moose skin boats.
Eliza and Sarah helped make the boats. It took two big bull moose
skins, sewed together. They used raw moose hide, not tanned, but
cut the hair off. They tied the hides on a birch wood frame with
strong caribou babiche. The bullet holes were sewed up tight and
covered with lots of moose tallow, which would get hard in the
water. They only used spruce pitch on birch bark boats. Inside they
used green spruce for crosspieces, but all the frame was birch. The
boat was large, maybe twenty feet long and could carry five dogs
and four or five people plus the meat and their camp. When they
went beaver trapping, they took all of their camp gear, ammunition
and dogs with them in the skin boats. They had to walk back, but
they got lots of beaver.

When Sarah's children were older, the teacher, Mrs. Hansen, talked
to their Dad and said they should be staying in Eagle during the
winter so the children could go to school. Sarah was happy to stay
home in the village with the children.

CHAPTER 12

FORT EGBERT
AND ARMY ACTIVITIES

The United States Army played an active role in the development of Alaska's Upper Yukon. Following the purchase of Alaska in 1867, the U.S. Army established headquarters at Sitka. The Commanding Officer, Brigadier-General Nelson A. Miles, was concerned about the lack of knowledge of the 577,390 square miles he was assigned to protect. It was practically an unexplored and unknown country, with little know of its topographical features, resources, climate or the number and character of its inhabitants.

One of the first military assignments was to send Captain Charles Raymond, an engineering officer in the U.S. Army to north-eastern Alaska to determine the site of the international boundary line at Fort Yukon. Besides determining the correct location of Fort Yukon, Captain Raymond also mapped the entire area in which he traveled, observed the resources of the Yukon and its tributaries and recorded the number and disposition of the native tribes in its vicinity.

In 1883, Lt. Schwatka and a party of seven men were sent to obtain additional military information regarding the interior of the Alaska Territory. They were mainly interested in the natives, their feelings towards the present government and the white people moving into that Territory, the amount and kind of weapons of war in their possession and the general character of the country to determine the best means of using and sustaining a military force, if one should be needed.

Hostilities did not occur with the native inhabitants of the Upper Yukon, but the gold discoveries in the North brought the return of the U.S. Army. During the summer of 1897, the War Department received conflicting reports as to the number of miners that were starving or threatened by lawlessness on the Yukon River. On August 4, 1897, Captain Ray and Lt. Richardson were directed to proceed to the Alaska gold fields to investigate, report and quell any disturbances.

Upon their arrival, Ray and Richardson found a difficult situation. The Yukon River was so low that fall, boats with the winter supplies could not go upriver beyond Fort Yukon which lead to the prospectors being threatened by both starvation and lawlessness. The army men were able to distribute adequate food to prevent the starvation and they recommended that army posts be established along the Yukon River to establish law and order. One of the sites they recommended was near the Canadian boarder at the mouth of Mission Creek which later became Fort Egbert.

After receiving Captain Ray's reports, the U.S. Congress approved the establishment of Forts along the Yukon River. In mid-March, 1899, Lt. Richardson with a detachment of 25 men was dispatched to Eagle where a military reservation was established which included the City of Eagle, giving the military authorities of the post full jurisdiction of that area. Richardson was instructed to begin construction of the initial phase of Fort Egbert. He was ordered to erect a barracks for 60 men and two officers and storehouses. On June 7, 1899, the post was officially named Fort Egbert in honor of Harry C. Egbert, an infantry colonel killed in action in the Philippines, March 26, 1899.

FORT EGBERT CONSTRUCTION BEGINS
Courtesy: National Archives

The initial Fort construction proceeded slowly. Land had to be cleared and temporary shelters set up. When Major Ray arrived later in the summer, it was clear that the pace of construction had to be stepped up in order to provide adequate shelter before winter. Ray even purchased an electric lighting outfit so that construction could continue during the dark winter months. Packers had arrived with horses, mules and cattle which needed to be housed. The wild cattle ran off and were never seen again. The horses and mules were in shelters by October. The enlisted men were in housing by November. At the year's end, a barracks, three officers quarters, post commissary, hospital, bakery, quarter master's warehouse and a sawmill had been built. With the exception of the corrugated

157

sawmill and bakery, all of the buildings were constructed of green logs. Wood hewers had been employed at a dollar an hour. Even at those wages, the force could not be kept full. The first buildings were poorly built, but subsequent ones were constructed with frame or milled lumber.

ARMY MESS HALL DURING FORT CONSTRUCTION
Courtesy: National Archives

Major Ray was named commander of the District of North Alaska, which included all of the country north of the 61st parallel.
He made his headquarters at Fort Egbert. Ray recommended that no more annual expeditions should be sent to Alaska to find an overland route to the interior of Alaska. Instead, he felt that all their energies should be spent on building a wagon road between Eagle City and Prince William Sound. While at Fort Egbert, Ray opened a wagon road from Eagle City to the Fortymile Country. Two properties in Eagle City received special treatment from Major Ray. On Dec. 14, 1899, he issued a revocable license to the super-intendents of the Catholic Mission and the Presbyterian Mission to

occupy several lots for church and mission purposes. Both licenses were approved by the Secretary of War in 1900.

In January 1900, a new army organization was established, named the Department of Alaska with its headquarters at St. MIchaels. Brig. General Randall was placed in charge.

CAPTAIN FARNSWORTH

Captain Farnsworth was sent to Fort Egbert in August 1900 to command the company stationed there, to complete the construction of the military post and to build a telegraph line. Charles Farnsworth, a graduate of West Point, was an able commander who quickly brought order out of chaos in spite of the mutinous drunken company he found on his hands.

The barracks was enlarged to accommodate 102 enlisted troops and eight new structures were erected by the years end. He next turned his attention to the construction of the telegraph line. They first built ten miles of telegraph line to the Canadian border, where it was hooked up the the Canadian line, through which messages could be sent to Skagway and hence by ship to Seattle.

The company was short on appropriate clothing for the entire first year, having only canvas fatigues and no woolen socks. Farnsworth felt the post was in a good location except for its proximity to a town where the disorderly saloons were a bad influence on the soldiers. In the horrible whiskey holes downtown, the soldiers became crazed by the vile stuff, got into fights and other trouble and finally deserted. To correct the situation, a post exchange was constructed without expense to the military, where beer was sold for 25 cents a glass. Two months after the post exchange had been in operation, there had been no desertions from the post. It was a heavy blow when the army bowed to the pressure of the Woman's Christian Temperance Union and closed all beer canteens at all the installations (Farnsworth, 1900).

The enlarged army post required many civilian employees. Many of these men brought their families with them and lived off the post in the City of Eagle. There were enough children in the combined communities, to warrant a school which was organized in 1901. Unofficial records for this period reported more social activities than military ones. The soldiers joined in the community social organizations, such as the Arctic Brotherhood, Improved Order of Redmen, Masonic Lodge and the Presbyterian church's weekly musical and reading room. Dances were held twice a month at the post for both communities. Military balls were held during the Christmas holidays at which formal attire was worn.

Captain Farnsworth had brought his wife and twelve year old son, Robert, to Fort Egbert with him, in addition to two servants. A piano was among their furnishings. Their son pursued his studies at home, reciting daily to his parents. He also had time to enjoy outdoor activities and especially enjoyed driving a dog team.

At first there were many complaints about the cold buildings. The logs for the buildings had been slabbed on three sides while still green and had warped out of shape. Though they had been caulked with oakum in September, the cracks soon showed up again. The

officers quarters were also cold, until they lined the walls with
tongue and groove boards over which cheese cloth and wall paper had
been applied, thus providing a pleasant affect with the painted
woodwork.

The Farnsworth family wrote that Fort Egbert was the most desirable
post in Alaska, as they enjoyed a number of pleasant people in town
and did not find the winter monotonous. Hops and socials were held
regularly and drills went on daily, so little difference could be
seen between this most northern post and any other one company post
in the states. About a dozen ladies of the town had weekly
afternoon parties which Mrs. Farnsworth enjoyed. The Wise Men's
Club met weekly during the winter to listen to essays written and
read by the member at whose house they met. The group was called
the 'Club of the Twelve Cranks' by the untutored rabble of the
town. During the spring they only met every two weeks for social
activities, dispensing with the wisdom part. One evening they met
at the Farnsworth home where the Captain turned the session into a
progressive card party complete with birch bark score cards. All
of the wives and daughters and other ladies of Eagle joined them
one evening as a surprise and served an elaborate lunch. They
dismissed at midnight and a crowd went duck hunting. For the next
few weeks, shotguns firing sounded like the 4th of July each night
between 11 p.m. and 3 a.m. (Farnsworth, 1900).

The officers enjoyed hunting and accompanied the post's hunting
parties to their camp 20 miles south of Eagle. As many as 52
caribou were killed in one day, which kept the garrison in meat
between purchases of pigs and cows. Besides his regular duties,
the Captain still found time to write an article on caribou hunting
and to gather specimens of birds and animals for the Smithsonian
Institution.

During the spring of 1901 Fort Egbert began its role in the
development of the Alaskan communication systems, the most
important historical event associated with the Fort. In February,
42 men began clearing a right-of-way for a telegraph line and a
trail for pack trains between Valdez and Eagle. During three weeks
in March, Captain Farnsworth examined the country for a practical
route for the telegraph line, pack trail and wagon road.

As spring arrived, Captain Farnsworth was feeling in A-1 shape and
wrote that since the post was now built, he wouldn't object to
staying another year. They had a good gym, baseball and football
fields and a library with 1200 volumes. The desertions were now
one quarter less than other companies. Unfortunately his wife,
Helen, suffered from frequent severe headaches and needed to have
her eyes examined outside. On June 1901, the command of Fort Egbert
was turned over to 1st Lt. Tillman. Farnsworth had placed a first
sergeant in charge of the telegraph line construction, but
recommended that a Signal Corps Officer be sent to take over this
responsibility.

In 1906, Fort Egbert hit its peak occupancy with ten officers, 147 enlisted men, 21 horses, 60 mules and 30 dogs. Not all of the men found the assignment at this northern post distasteful. In fact some liked it so much, that every two years when their company was ready to transfer, they would resign and join the new outfit coming in. They hoped to remain in Alaska until they retired from the Army and become old timers. One of those men was Private Samuel Woodfill who arrived at Fort Egbert in 1904 and managed to remain there for eight years.

Woodfill recalled that Alaska hit him just right; the longer he stayed the better he liked it. Luckily the first winter was the mildest of his four hitches, described by the old sourdoughs as nothing but shirt-sleeve weather. The soldiers were well dressed with heavy red wool underwear and thick woolen uniforms. The fatigue uniforms were canvas lined with woolen blanket cloth and for garrison duty they had the heaviest kind of woolen mackinaws.

ACTIVITIES IN FORT EGBERT GYMNASIUM
Courtesy: Eagle Historical Society

The shoes were made of felt; for rough work they put moose skin moccasins over the felt shoes with two or three extra pairs of wool socks underneath. They had muskrat fur caps. The second winter was the coldest of the eight Woodfill spent in Alaska. The Fort ran out of wood halfway through the winter when the thermometers recorded minus 72 degrees F. and stayed right there. Five men froze to death during that winter inside a radius of a hundred miles from the Fort.

The soldiers were always busy and never had time to get lonesome even though they were thousands of miles away from civilization. They were put to work erecting many new log buildings. One of the structures they built was a large gymnasium. Woodfill's job was driving a team; his first experience skinning mules included learning a new language. Soon spring arrived and the river ice broke up. When the ice went out, everyone enjoyed the biggest holiday period of the year and a lot of money changed hands, betting on the breakup.

There was no lack of gambling. Alaska was wide open, with a choice of craps, poker, faro, roulette, black-jack of chuck-luck, a game the old timers played with five dice. The professional shysters were as thick as mosquitos on a moose. A prospector could come in with a whole season's gold pannings in a sack and his whole stake could be gone before morning.

Woodfill served his turn at a telegraph line cabin. Another summer he was delegated to the fish camp, a big fish wheel at the mouth of Mission Creek on the Yukon River. He lived alone in a tent and caught salmon for the mess hall and winter food for the dog teams. Each morning, after a swim in the river, he cleaned the ton of fish and took them back to the fort in a rowboat. After that, he would hunt in the hills for a few days until the company mess needed another mess of fish and he would clean out the fish wheel boxes again.

The private spent his spare time practicing at the rifle range. Shooting seemed to come natural to him and he became a sharp shooter. He loved to hunt the big game. During the summer a detachment from the Fort would always be stationed at a military hunting camp, bringing back game by pack train. After the novelty of the hunting trips wore off, the hunting simmered down to six men who were really keen about it. Woodfill was detailed to the hunting camp as a sort of permanent fixture to break in all the new fellows and show them the country. It was hard rough work, but he loved the thrill of hunting big game which required being sure on the trigger and without nerves.

Even though Woodfill and his friends had no intention of leaving Alaska, word was received that Fort Egbert was to be abandoned. The gold rush was over; no longer was there a need to keep law and order or to make life easier for the prospectors on the trail of

gold. Eagle was so dead, it was almost respectable. By 1910 the
wireless telegraph began to supplant the land and sea cable system
and no longer required the personnel to maintain the old telegraph
line. In 1910 the Army reduced the Fort Egbert complement to two
officers and 35 men. The next year the infantry departed, leaving
a small Signal Corps detachment to man the five-kilowatt wireless
station and a small hospital detachment remained to provide the
only medical care available.

COMPLETED FORT EGBERT
Courtesy: National Archives

There are not only buildings left at Fort Egbert, but also many
memories. The last Fort Egbert soldier to return to Eagle was
Henry David McCary, who at 16 years of age had served as a company
bugler from 1908-1910. In sharing his memories 62 years later, he
said, "I lived in a world of pure fantasy. In the evening when I
would sound taps, I noted that many men would open their windows to
listen. The bugle's notes bounced off the wall of the granite
bluffs 1,000 yards distance and then seemed to circle over the
frozen Yukon creating a five-fold echo. I thought I was communi-
cating with angels, or with soldiers who had died in battle
(McCary, 1969, EHS Archives). One must experience the rare
northern atmosphere and the bright scintillating northern lights,
to fully appreciate those vivid memories of Bugler McCary's musical
fantasy, which brought him back to the scene of his soldier's life
in the Upper Yukon.

CHAPTER 13

ARMY COMMUNICATIONS

WAMCATS
Washington-Alaska Military Cable and Telegraph System
1900

One of the charges given to the U.S. Army stationed in Alaska, was
to establish communications. This became critical during the 1896
gold rush when the Army built Forts along the Yukon River. It took
six months or more to get a letter from the Yukon to Washington,
D.C. and a response back. Brig. General Randall recommend in Jan.
27, 1900 that a telegraph line should be built between Fort St.
Michael, Cape Nome, the posts along the Yukon and Valdez. He
referred this project to the Cheif Signal Officer, General Greely
for estimates. Congress appropriated $450,550 on May 26, 1900.

Fort Egbert at Eagle became the base for building one of the first
telegraph lines, a twelve mile segment which ran along the Yukon
River eastward to the Canadian boundary. Plans were soon developed
to build the segment of the Washington-Alaska Military Cable and
Telegraph System, an All-American telegraph line, directly from
Fort Egbert to Valdez. Brigadier Gen. A.W. Greely, Signal Corps
Commanding Officer in Washington, D.C., felt that the construction
of the new line was going far to slowly. He sent a 21-year old
family friend, by the name of Billy Mitchell, to Fort Egbert to
investigate the situation in 1901. When Lt. Mitchell reported back
that the line could be completed quickly, Gen. Greely ordered him
to return and build it.

Mitchell made his base at Fort Egbert between 1901 and 1903. After
completing the line to the Tanana River, he continued his work on
the 204 mile segment of the Goodpaster line, all under difficult
conditions. The final work consisted of joining the Fort Egbert-
Fort Liscum line to the one from Fort St. Michael. After incredibly
hard work, Mitchell met Lt. Gibbons near the Salcha River on June
27, 1903, making the final connection to the trans-Alaska telegraph
system.

The men of the U.S. Army Signal Corps had completed the 1,506 miles
of overland lines from Nome and St. Michaels to Valdez and a few
hundred miles of submarine cable in just three years, one month and
one day; a truly impressive achievement against overwhelming odds.

Completion of the telegraph line, did not end the military's work.
Stationed at log cabins spaced 40 miles apart, detachments of
soldiers maintained the line. Through blizzards, summer heat and
mosquitoes, forest fires and storms, these soldiers kept the line
operating. Maintaining the telegraph line was lonely and monotonous
duty at low wages.

In 1907 the Signal Corps began to use wireless or radio equipment and by the end of 1915, WAMCATS had reduced its land lines to 848 miles. No longer needed to maintain the telegraph lines, the Infantry Company left Fort Egbert in 1911, leaving a small Signal Corps detachment to man the new five-kilowatt wireless station. This station, which was located on 'telegraph hill', burned to the ground in 1921, but the Fort Egbert radio station was reestablished

Freighting Telegraph Supplies on Yukon River
Courtesy: Eagle Historical Society

in the town in October 1922. This was manned by a single Signal Corps operator until 1934 when the Army closed this station and turned over the operation of the radio to the Northern Commercial Company store.

By the end of June 1940, radio had entirely replaced the cables. Located in a mountain valley, Eagle has very poor radio reception. Each evening residents strained to hear 'Caribou Chatter' or 'Mukluk News' to receive personal messages.

Satellites brought a bright new future for Eagle's communication. In 1973, the first satellite dish was placed in Eagle Village for medical messages. In 1982 Alaska purchased space on one of the satellites, which provided Eagle residents their present bush television station and long distance telephones.

In 1901, the U.S. Signal Corps sent Billy Mitchell, a 21 year old lieutenant to Alaska to build a particularly difficult section of the telegraph line. It was to link the Army Forts in the District of Alaska to the outside world.

LT. WM. MITCHELL IN EAGLE
Photo Courtesy: National Archives

Lt. Mitchell was born December 29, 1879, the eldest son of a wealthy and politically prominent Wisconsin family. He grew up on the family estate near Milwaukee, surrounded by horses and dogs. Billy's father, John Lendrum Mitchell, was serving as an U.S. Senator when the United States declared war on Spain in April 1898. The younger Mitchell, then 18 years old and in his third year at Columbia University, Washington, D.C. (now George Washington University), immediately enlisted in the 1st Wisconsin Infantry, the outfit in which his father had served during the Civil War. Seven days later, he was on his way to Florida and had been commissioned a 2nd lieutenant, the youngest in the army. Mitchell soon transferred to the Signal Corps. Before his first summer in uniform ended, he was in command of a company which was sent to the Philippines.

After combat in the Philippines, Mitchell soon became bored with garrison life at Fort Myer and considered resigning his commission. Then he was confronted with a new challenge. Gold had been discovered in Alaska in 1896. With it came an influx of adventurerers from all over the world without an existence of any law and order.

He was soon sent to Alaska to investigate the slow progress on the construction of the proposed telegraph line. After surveying the projected routes, Mitchell reported that no work was being done in the winter and in the summer, the Alaska muskeg was too soft for horses to pull or carry significant loads. The solution which he proposed was to position the wire, poles and other equipment and supplies in the winter while the ground was frozen, then erect the line in the summer. Old Alaska hands told Mitchell it was impossible to work in the minus 50 to 70 degree
winter temperatures. He didn't believe them.

Mitchell, who began the work with few instructions and no superior officer to whom he could turn, wisely consulted miners, trappers, Indians--anyone who could teach him how to survive and work in the Alaskan winters. He spent the first winter surveying a route from Fort Egbert to the Tanana River.

After the survey was completed, Mitchell placed caches of supplies and shelters for the horses and men along the route at fifteen mile intervals. Mitchell invented a new kind of shoe for the horses, devised Arctic clothing for the men, hunted most of the food for his 45 men, concocted a concentrated ration for the trail and according to letters home, fell in love with Alaska's wilderness.

Mitchell took the thermometers away from his men as they were afraid to go out when it was 60 to 70 degrees below zero. They had orders to work every day regardless of the temperature. They did and they thrived on it. Not one of Mitchell's men fell victim to gold fever and deserted, though desertion was common among garrison troops at the Forts.

Summers, with the clouds of mosquitos, were worse than winters.

Smudges had to be built to keep the mosquitos away. Horses would not leave the smoke to graze and had to be driven out. Whatever command he held, Mitchell always felt that his men were the finest in the Army. The feelings were mutual; the men working on the telegraph line looked forward to Mitchell's arrival, surprising him with home made Christmas gifts and other items.

Despite the obstacles, Mitchell's men completed the line from Fort Egbert to the Tanana River in fifteen months, linking up on August 24, 1902 with the line coming northward from Valdez. Mitchell then turned his men to the west, down the unexplored Tanana River. On June 27, 1903 Mitchell made the connection between his line and the one built westward from Nome and St. Michael. The telegraph line, which was open to civilian as well as military use, was a major factor in the development of Alaska. Billy Mitchell went home, the youngest captain in the Army.

CHAPTER 14

ROALD AMUNDSEN

As early as the sixteenth century, many countries had been searching for the elusive Northwest Passage as a shorter route to send their valuable furs to the Chinese market. Numerous expeditions had been sent without success; some met tragic endings. It remained unknown until Roald Amundsen sailed his ship through this ice bround passage in 1905.

As a youth, Roald Amundsen dreamed of becoming an Arctic explorer to join the search for the Northwest Passage. For his preparation, he spent two years as an ordinary seaman on an Arctic sealing vessel to qualify for his skipper's papers. After listening to many scientists arguing whether or not the magnetic poles were fixed or whether they moved, he was fired by a new idea; if he could discover the secret of the North Magnetic Pole, that would be a coup almost equal to the conquest of the Passage. In 1900, he sought out a German professor to teach him the theory and practice of magnetic observation.

During the winter of 1900-1901, Amundsen bought a small 32-year-old wooden herring boat which he named the GJOA. He planned to have a small hand-picked six-man crew who would wear native clothing, sleep in native snow houses, learn to handle and drive dogs and use them with skis. He even rejected commercial pemmican in favor of his own recipe.

At last he was ready to go. He had everything he needed except money. On June 15, 1903, loaded with five years provisions and equipment, he and his crew of six cast off from the docks on the stroke of midnight to escape his creditors. Within two months he was in the heart of the Arctic archipelago where he found a small suitable harbor. They anchored and christened it Gjoa Haven. It would be their home for the next two years, in an effort to locate the North Magnetic Pole.

After they had constructed two buildings for magnetic observation, a band of Nitsilik Eskimos arrived. The two groups developed an affectionate bond and the band of Eskimos moved to Gjoa Haven in a body. The Eskimos taught them how to dress, build houses, obtain food, travel and most of all, the value of patience in the Arctic.

Two winters at Gjoa Haven required monumental patience. When Amundsen reached the spot where James Clark Ross had located the north pole, he discovered that the pole had moved some 30 miles. Many considered his discovery that the pole was not fixed, was his major achievement. Amundsen also learned that the un-navigated portion of the Northwest Passage was no more than 150 miles as the crow flew from his present location.

On June 1, 1905, the Amundsen party continued on their journey. The Gjoa groped its way through the fog into the shallow, island-dotted strait guided by some of the natives in their kayaks. No white man had sailed through these totally unknown, totally unpredictable waters before. Amundsen wrote, "We bungled through zigzaging as if we were drunk. The lead continued to fly up and down and the lookout in the crow's nest was flinging his arms about like a maniac indicating sudden shifts to port and starboard. It was like sailing through an uncleared field "

Somehow the Gjoa made it through and anchored in Cambridge Bay on August 17, 1905 where they met whaling ships. While frozen in their third winter at Hershel Island, Amundsen met a Captain Mogg whose whaling boat had been destroyed in the ice. Mogg was making plans to return to San Francisco to obtain another ship; he had hired an Eskimo couple with a dog team to take him as far as Fort Yukon. Amundsen joined this party in order to obtain some medical advice for one of his sick crew members. When he reached Fort Yukon, he was told that telegraph services were available in Eagle City. Wanting to send a message back to Norway, he continued his journey 350 miles up the Yukon River by dog team.

AMUNDSEN AT EAGLE

Amundsen arrived in Eagle City on Dec. 5, 1905 with the thermometer reading 60 degrees below zero. The tall gaunt stranger entered the commercial store looking weary and bedraggled and purchased supplies from the Northern Commercial agent, Frank H. Smith. The clerks thought he was just another discouraged prospector in from the creeks and no one paid him any attention. He was dead broke, not even having the price of a telegram which he wanted to send. It was in seeking permission to send this telegram without cost that his identity became known. He was the great explorer, Captain Amundsen, who had mushed down from the Arctic Coast where his ship was icebound at King's Point, one thousand miles to the northeast. He was directed to the telegraph office at Fort Egbert where he sent a 3,000 word telegram to Nansen, at Christiana, Norway. He wanted to let his family know he was alive and healthy and also to ask his brother to send him some money. The weather was so cold, the telegraph line kept breaking, causing Amundsen to wait several weeks for his answers. Finally the Bank of Seattle wired him the funds which he had requested and a Seattle newspaper sent him news of his family and country.

Amundsen remained in Eagle for two months. He boarded with the Frank Smith family, who lived in the Northern Commercial Co. mess house where they had extra rooms and a Chinese cook. He joined in many of the winter social functions, gave speeches for the residents in the Fort Egbert gymnasium and enjoyed a short rest. In February 1906, Mr. Smith outfitted him with dogs, sleds and supplies and Amundsen returned to his ship. Nine months later on September 1, 1906, his party reached Nome, completing the first

171

ROALD AMUNDSEN ARRIVING IN EAGLE
Courtesy: Johnson Collection, EHS

voyage from the Atlantic to the Pacific via the Arctic Ocean.

Frank Smith met Amundsen in San Francisco and assisted him in finding a storage place to leave the Gjoa. After Amundsen returned to Norway and had reported to the Norwegian King, Frank Smith was awarded an honorary Knighthood of St. Olaf for the assistance which he had given Roald Amundsen in Eagle City and San Francisco.

By bringing his ship through the hitherto un-navigated link in the
Northwest Passage, Amundsen had shown that there was no practical
passage for large ships. Only a tiny craft of shallow draft, such
as the Gjoa, could hope to make it through Simpson Strait. Because
of his careful study and planning, his crew had not suffered
scurvy, starvation, exhaustion or semi-madness which had afflicted
the previous earlier explorers. Amundsen had made it look so easy,
he has not been given the acclaim which he deserved.

Roald Amundsen continued his explorations, being the first to reach
the South Pole on December 16, 1912. He met his death in 1925 in an
airplane crash while searching for the lost explorer, Umbert
Nobile, who had been flying a dirigible.

Eagle City honors this international hero with a monument in their
Amundsen Park and the main street entering town has been named
Amundsen Avenue. A beautiful model (1/4 inch=1 foot) of the Gjoa is
now on exhibit in the Eagle's museums. In 1995 and 1996, Suzan
Amundsen, a relative of Roald Amundsen, presently living near the
Fairbanks area, mushed into Eagle City while participating in the
Yukon Quest Dog Race. So there are still Amundsens mushing their
dog teams down the Yukon River to Eagle.

CHAPTER XV

EAGLE CITY 1997

This is the year the residents of Eagle City are looking forward to a centennial celebration of the founding of their city 1897-1997. One hundred years and it never became a ghost town, as many of the early gold rush towns did. There was always a nucleus of people who remained and kept the city operating. World War II (1941-1945) came the closest to depopulating the area when gold mining was shut down. Even then the nine remaining residents maintained the city council and the community.

By 1953 with the opening of the Taylor Highway, which connects Eagle City to the Alcan Highway, the population began to increase. Though there is no major economic base, people are drawn to Eagle by its setting, tranquility and remoteness. If to many people indicate an interest in moving to Eagle, residents have been heard to tell them it can get very cold in winter and the mosquitos can become fierce during the summer. During the late 60's and until the mid 80's many young people were living up and down the Yukon River using Eagle as a base (McPhee, 1976). Few of the early residents along the rivers had bothered to obtain deeds to the property they used and lived on. Thus there was very little private land for these 'river people' so most of them were living on public land which had been withdrawn from entry by the Department of Interior. The land withdrawal remained in place until selections had been completed and the land surveyed for the natives and Federal agencies as permitted by ANSCA (Native Land Claims) and the State of Alaska (statehood act). The result of ANSCA was that all of the land remotely close to Eagle was transferred to either the natives (Indian allotments, Eagle Village or Doyon - part of the Tanana Chiefs Corporation) or the National Park Service, forcing the young 'river people' off the river. A two mile buffer zone was established around the perimeter of Eagle City; this land was deeded to the State of Alaska. Eagle City had indeed become the JEWEL ON THE YUKON.

By 1997, the population of Eagle City had gradually increased to 164. The public road had been extended five miles beyond Eagle Village to provide access to the Indian allotments. Many residents were able to purchase larger acreage than the city lots from the Indians and moved out of town on roads adjacent to the city.

The residents of Eagle have maintained many of the original buildings. The Eagle Historical Society & Museums (EHSM) and City of Eagle have been instrumental in restoring six of the large public buildings (1900-1901) and have put them into use. 23, 1996. The original city hall (1901) is still in use by the City government, with a log addition for their modern office equipment. The first school building (1903) has become the recreational center for Eagle, with playground equipment, booths for the 4th of July and serves as the check point for the Yukon Quest and Percy DeWolfe Memorial dog races. The original church is still in use, though the rectory burned to the ground Dec. The Improved Order of Redmen Lodge (1904) is being restored and used by EHSM for community functions and office space. Paulson & Ott's store (1898) has been reopened as the Eagle Commercial Co.

Several of the original residences have been restored and are back in use, especially by summer residents. Many other original buildings still stand and are in need of restoration. Most of the newer buildings resemble the early architecture, so that they compliment the first structures. It is no wonder, that the AP reporter wrote, "Original cabins still stand among the birch groves, giving Eagle the feel of a freshly opened time capsule."

Not only have many of the 100-year-old buildings remained the same, but also many of the activities of the residents. They still enjoy fish from the river and wild game from the woods (mainly moose, caribou and bear). Boating on the Yukon River and it's tributaries is still a summer time activity. Dog teams are popular, though most residents use snow machines or four-wheelers. Skiing and snow shoeing have become more recreational rather than a necessity. Occasionally a horse or two is brought to Eagle. A moderate amount of trapping still occurs, even with the smaller market and lower prices for the furs. Many of the furs are made into hats by the local ladies and some still make skin boots for winter use. Large gardens are still a necessity for both vegetables and flowers. Reading remains popular, as noted by the heavy use of the public library. The hand-dug well (1903) is still the source of water for the residents without private wells. The trails and roads continue to be dirt without any surfacing. Tourists continue to find Eagle. A hundred years ago, the tourists arrived on the sternwheelers. Today they drive the highway, float down the river, fly on commercial flights or privately owned planes, arrive on GreyLine tour buses or Holland-America's (Westours) tour boat from Dawson. Visitors are drawn by the setting of the community, friendliness of the residents, plus the walking tour of the five museums with their excellent exhibits which interpret the history of the area and the lifestyle and occupations of the early residents.

Some businesses have remained and others disappeared. Two grocery stores, one hardware store, a gun shop, pool hall, jewelry and gift stores meet resident's and visitor's needs. A motel, rental cabins, restaurant and two bed and breakfast establishments have replaced the roadhouses. Wood cutters are fewer, but still exist. Gone are the bars (Eagle is a damp community), blacksmith shop and tin smith shop.

So what has changed over Eagle's 100 year history?
    Taylor Highway into Eagle now provides summer access by road, though all the road and trails remain gravel.
    Electricity generated locally replaced the kerosene lamps.

Digital oil heaters replaced some of the wood burning heaters.

Long-distance telephones (via satellite) have replaced the early telegrams.

Television dishes now appear in residential yards.

Videos checked out from the library replace movie nights at the Courthouse or library.

Computers in the homes and business are common place.

E-mail replaces the dog-team mail men.

Airplanes bring passengers, mail and freight plus medivacing the sick and injured.

Cold weather months are enhanced by the new insulting materials available for clothing and buildings; a great improvement over the 'ticking material' parkas and sawdust in the walls papered with cheese cloth and newspapers.

Steel roofing has replaced most of the pole and moss roofs, and the later flattened kerosene can shingles.

Many of the out houses have been replaced by the modern conveniences of in-door bathrooms and septic tanks. Eagle is not planning any community water or sewer services; each resident provides their own source of water

Plastic water buckets and tanks have replaced the empty kerosene water cans and wooden tanks.

The volunteer fire department has fire and water trucks, replacing the bucket brigade.

The road to Eagle now requires service stations and repair garages for all the automobiles, trucks and graders for the roads and air field.

Jet motors for the boats replaces lining them up the river.

New multimillion dollar school building houses educational and recreational activities and includes school bus service.

Garden rototillers replaced the horse drawn plow.

Living in Eagle today makes one fully appreciate and admire the hardiness of the early pioneers and the lives which they lived. One does not hear many present residents complain about the changes which have occurred over the past hundred years.

Eagle today offers a simpler life style, one of independence and freedom, as well as appreciation of the beautiful landscape and the power of Mother Nature. How fortunate one feels, to sit at a dining room table and watch the great Yukon River flow by with a full moon rising over the mountains in the background, or on a clear cold night to watch the northern lights shimmering and dancing about in the sky, which especially impressed the author, James Michener, during his 1984 visit to Eagle. To watch the strength of the river as large chunks of ice tumble over each other during the 'break-up', can be a very humbling experience.

BIBLIOGRAPHY

BOOKS

Adney, Tappan. The Klondike Stampede. Harper's, New York 1900.

Amundsen, Roald. My Life as an Explorer. Doubleday Doran & Co. 1928.

Andrews, Clarence L. The Story of Alaska. Caxton Printers, Idaho. 1944.

Atwood, Evangeline. Frontier Politics. Binford & Mort, Portland. 1968.

Balcolm, Mary. The Catholic Church in Alaska. Adams Press, Illinois. 1970.

Bancroft, Herbert Howe. History of Alaska 1739-1885. A. L. Bancroft Co., California. 1886.

Barnett, Dave. The Upper Yukon - Wilderness Hunting. Amwell Press, New Jersey. 1983.

Berton, Pierre. Arctic Grael.

--------------- Klondike. McClelland & Steward, Toronto. 1972.

Burke, Clara Heintz. Doctor Hap. Coward-McCann, New York. 1961.

Chase, William H. Pioneers of Alaska. Burton, Kansas City. 1951.

Coates, Ken & Bill Morrison. The Sinking of the Princess Sophia. University of Alaska Press, Fairbanks. 1990.

Cole, Terrence. Crooked Creek. University of Alaska Press, Fairbanks. 1991.

Crow, John R. & Phillip P. Obley. Handbook of North American Indians, vol. 6. Smithsonian Institute, Washington, D.C. 1981.

Crowe, Keith J. A History of the Original Peoples of Northern Canada. Arctic Institute of North America. McGill-Queen's University Press, Montreal, P.Q. 1974.

Cruikshank, Julie. Their Own Yukon. Yukon press, Whitehorse, Yukon. 1975.

Davis, Mary Lee Sourdough Gold. W.A. Wilde Co., Boston. 1933.

Dawson Indian Band. <u>Han Indians, People of the River.</u> College
    Printers, Vancouver, B.C. 1988.

DeHart, Don & Vangie. <u>Guide of the Yukon River.</u> Cheyenne Litho
    Inc., Wyoming. 1971.

Gates, Michael. <u>Gold at Fortymile Creek.</u> UBC Press, Vancouver.
    1994.

Greely, Major-General A. W. <u>Handbook of Alaska.</u> Charles Scribner's
    Sons, New York. 1919.

Hamilton, Walter R. <u>Yukon Story.</u> Mitchell, Vancouver. 1967.

Haynes, Terry L. <u>They Didn't Come in Four-Wheel Drives: An
    Introduction to Fortymile History.</u> Western Interstate
    Commission for Higher Education, Boulder, CO. 1976.

Heller, Herbert L. <u>Sourdough Sagas.</u> Ballantine Books, New York.
    1967.

Hunt, William R. <u>North of 53</u>. Macmillan Publishing Co., New York.
    1974.

Jackson, Sheldon. <u>Alaska</u>. Dodd, Mead & Co., New York. 1880.

Jenkins, Thomas. <u>The Man of Alaska: Peter Trimble Rowe</u>.
    Morehouse-Gorham, New York. 1953.

Kirk, James W. <u>Pioneer Life in the Yukon Valley, Alaska.</u>
    Presbyterian Church, Buffalo. 1935.

Kitchener, L.D. <u>Flag Over the North: Northern Commercial Co.</u>
    Superior, Seattle. 1954.

Knutson, Arthur E. <u>Sternwheels on the Yukon.</u> Knutson Enterprises,
    Kirkland, WA. 1979.

Kosuta, Kathy. <u>Han Indians</u>. College Printers, Vancouver, B.C. 1988.

Lazell, J. Arthur. <u>Alaskan Apostle: The Life Story of Sheldon
    Jackson.</u>Harper & Bros., New York. 1960.

Lyman L. Woodman Lt. Colonel, USAF-retired. <u>Duty Station Northwest</u>
    Vol. I. Alaska Historical Society, Anchorage, Alaska. 1996.

McClellan, Catherine. <u>My Old People Say.</u> National Museum of Man,
    Ottowa. 1975.

McCombe, R.S. <u>Alaska on the Cover.</u> Delta Junction, Alaska. 1983.

McLain, John Scudder. <u>Alaska and the Klondike.</u> McClure, Phillips
     & Co. New York. 1905.

McPhee, John. <u>Coming into the Country</u>. Farrar, Straus & Giroux, New
     York. 1977.

McQueston, Leroy N. <u>Recollections of Leroy N. McQueston: Life in
     the Yukon 1871-1885.</u> Yukon Order of Pioneers, Dawson, Yukon
     1952.

Mercier, Francois Xavier. <u>Recollections of the Youkon: 1868-1885.</u>
     Alaska Historical Society, Anchorage, Alaska 1986.

Mitchell, Ruth. <u>My Brother Bill.</u> Harcourt, Brace. 1953.

Mitchell, William. <u>Opening of Alaska.</u> Cook Inlet Historical Society
     Anchorage, Alaska. 1981.

Naske, Claus-M. <u>Paving Alaska's Trails.</u> University Press of
America.
     1986. p.1.

Nelson, Richard K. <u>Hunters of the Northern Forest.</u> University of
     Chicago Press, Chicago. 1973.

Newell, Gordon. <u>Duty, Honor, Country: George H. McManus.</u> Evergreen
     Press Ltd. Vancouver. (n.d.)

Ogilvie, William. <u>Early Days on the Yukon.</u> John Lane Co., New York.
     1913.

Osgood, Cornelius. <u>Han Indians.</u> Yale University Press, New Haven.
     1971.

Paul, Louise & Eliza Malcolm. <u>Raven Tales</u>. Eagle Village 1986.

Potter, Jean. <u>The Flying North.</u> Macmillan Company, New York. 1947.

Pyle, Ernie. <u>Home Country.</u> Wm. Sloane, Assoc., New York. 1947

Savage, A. H. <u>Dogsled Apostles.</u> Sheed & Ward, New York. 1942.

Schmitter, Ferdinand. <u>Upper Yukon Native Customs & Folk-lore.</u> Eagle
     Historical Society. Eagle, Alaska 1985.

Schwatka, Frederick. <u>A Summer in Alaska</u>. J. W. Henry, St. Louis,
     Missouri. 1893.

Scott, Elva R. <u>Eagle Schools Eighty Years 1901-1981.</u> Alaska
     Historical Commission. Anchorage, Alaska. 1981.

--------- Health History of the Upper Yukon. Alaska
     Historical Society, Anchorage, Alaska. 1983.

--------- Historic Eagle and its People. Eagle Historical Society
     Eagle City, Alaska 1996.

-------- Life in the Northern Army. Argus Printing Co.,
     Hillsboro, Oregon. 1986.

Sheldon, Charles. Wilderness of the Upper Yukon. Copp Clark Co.,
     Toronto. 1911.

Shore, Evelyn Berglund. Born on Snowshoes. Houghton Mifflin Co.,
     Boston. 1954.

Steinbright, Jan, editor. From Skins, Trees, Quills and Beads: The
     Work of Nine Athabascans. Institute of Alaska Native Arts,
     Fairbanks.

Stuck, Hudson. Alaskan Missions of the Episcopal Church. Shorey
     Book Store, Seattle. 1968.

-------- Ten Thousand Miles with a Dogsled. Charles Scribner's
     Sons, New York. 1914.

Thomas, Lowell, Woodfill of the Regulars. Doubleday, Doran & Co.,
     New York. 1929.

Van Stone, James W. Athapaskan Adaptations. Aldine Publishing Co.,
     Chicago. 1974.

Walker, Franklin. Jack London & the Klondike. Huntington Library,
     Pasadena. 1978.

Weimer, M.D.K. True Story of the Alaska Gold Field. (n.p.) 1903.

Wharton, David. The Alaska Gold Rush. Indiana University Press.
     1972.

Whymper, Frederick. Travel and Adventure in the Territory of
     Alaska. Harper & Brother, New York. 1871.

Wickersham, James. Old Yukon: Tales, Trails, Trials. Washington Law
     Book Co., Washington, D.C. 1938.

Wilson, Clifford. Campbell of the Yukon. Macmillan, Toronto. 1970.

Woodman, Lyman L. Duty Station Northwest: Vol. I. Alaska Historical
     Society, Anchorage, Alaska 1996.

ARTICLES

Couch, Jim. "Sixty Years a Pioneer: Bob Steel." The Alaska
     Sportsman. March 1957.

----------. "The Wizard of Eagle: E. A. Robertson, Nimrod."
     The Alaska Sportsman. February 1957.

Darrell, Cash J. "Eagle on the Yukon". The Alaska Life. December
     1946.

DeArmond, Robert. "Gold on the Fortymile." The Alaska Journal.
     Spring 1973.

Hansen, Borghilde. "Ice Jam." The Alaska Sportsman. August 1959.

Hunt, William R. "A Soldier on the Yukon: Captain Farnsworth".
     Journal of the West. April 1971.

Mitchell, William. "Building the Alaskan Telegraph System."
     National Geographic. September 1904.

Renner, Louis L., S.J. "Father Francis M. Monroe, S.J." The Alaska
     Magazine. April 1979.

Scott, Elva R. "Alaska Educational Systems in Action at Eagle,
     Alaska, 1901-1981." Education in Alaska's Past. Alaska
     Historical Society. 1983.

--------"Arctic Explorer leaves imprint on Eagle." Fairbanks Daily
     News. Heartland. October 6, 1996.

--------"Bringing the Mail was Dog-hard Work." Fairbanks Daily
     News. Interior Scrapbook. February 18, 1990.

--------"Eagle City felt first effects of early Alaskan Aviation."
     Alaska Flyer. Anchorage. June 1989.

-------editor. Eagle Historical Papers. 2 volumes. Eagle
     Historical Society, Eagle, Alaska. 1971.

-------editor. "Historical Articles". Eagle Wireless. Eagle
     Historical Society Newsletter. Eagle, Alaska. 1975-1990.

Van Dusen, William. "The Man Who Ate the Bear: Nimrod." True
     Magazine. (n.d.).

Winnipeg, C. Parnell. "Campbell of the Yukon." The Beaver. 1942.

GOVERNMENT PUBLICATIONS

Abercrombie, 2nd Lt. W.E. "A Supplementary Expedition into the
    Copper River Valley, 1884". Narratives of Explorations in
    Alaska. Government Printing Office, Washington D.C. 1900.
    p. 383.

-------------"A Military Reconnaissance of the Copper River Valley,
    1898". Narratives of Explorations in Alaska. Government
    Printing Office, Washington, D.C. 1900. p. 563.

Allen, Lt. Henry T. 2nd Cavalry, USA. "A Military Reconnaissance
    of the Copper River Valley. 1885" Narratives of Explorations
    in Alaska. Government Printing Office, Washington, D.C. 1900.
    p. 411.

Babcock, 1st Lt. Walter C., 8th U.S. Cavalry. "The Trans-Alaskan
    Military Road". Narratives of Explorations in Alaska.
    Government Printing Office, Washington, D.C. 1900 p. 770.

Georgeson, C.C. Agricultural Investigations in Alaska. 1899 Report.

----------- Alaska Agricultural Experimental Stations. Annual
    Report 1909.

Gillette, Edward. "The Great Copper River Region." Narratives of
    Exploration in Alaska. Government Printing Office. Washington,
    D.C. 1900. p. 807.

Murray, Alexander Hunter. Journal of the Yukon 1947-48. ed. by L.J.
    Burpee, Government Printing Bureau, Ottawa. 1910.

Pathfinder of Alaska. "History of WAMCAT". Department of Interior.
    1925.

Quirk, William A. III. Historical Aspects of the Building of the
    WAMCAT. U. S. Department of Interior, Bureau of Land
    Management. 1974.

Ray, Captain P. H. "Relief of the Destitute in the Gold Fields,
    1897." Narratives of Explorations in Alaska. Government
    Printing Office. Washington, D.C. 1900. p. 497.

Raymond, C. R. "Reconnaissance of the Yukon River, 1869".
Compilation of Narratives of Explorations in Alaska. U.S.
    Government Printing Office, Washington, D.C. 1871.

Rice, John F., "From Valdez to Eagle City." Narratives of
    Explorations in Alaska. Government Printing Office,
    Washington, D.C. 1900. p. 784.

Richardson, Brigadier General W. P. Alaska Board of Road
    Commissioners Reports 1917. Government Printing Office.
    Washington, D.C. 1918.

Schwatka, Frederick. <u>Report of a Military Reconnaissance in Alaska.</u>
    U. S. Government Printing Office. Washington, D.C. 1885.

Shinkwin, Andrews, Sackett & Kroul. <u>Fort Egbert and the Eagle
    Historic District.</u> Bureau of Land Management, Tok, Alaska.
    1978.

United States 55th Congress 2d Session
    House of Representatives. Document #285.
    "Additional Military Post in Alaska." 1898

    House of Representatives. Document #14
    "Alaska Gold Fields." 1897.
    United States Printing Office. Washington, D. C.

United States 55th Congress 3d Session
    House of Representatives Document #244.
    "Relief of People in the Yukon River Country." 1899.
    United States Printing Office. Washington, D.C.

United States Senate Report #1023. <u>Compilation of Narratives of
    Exploration in Alaska.</u> 2 volumes. United States Printing
    Office. Washington, D.C.

Wells, E. Hazard, "Up and Down the Yukon." <u>Narratives of
    Explorations in Alaska.</u> Government Printing Office.
    Washington, D.C. 1900. p. 511.

UNPUBLISHED DIARIES AND MANUSCRIPTS

Andrews, Elizabeth. "Archeological Perceptions of Early Contact:
    Han Indians at Eagle." Eagle Historical Society Symposium.
    Eagle, Alaska. July 1986.

Bowers, Peter M. & David M. Hoch. "An Archeological Reconnaissance
    of the Copper Creek Drainage, Upper Charley River Area, East-
    Central, Alaska." National Park Service, University of Alaska,
    Fairbanks, Alaska. November 1976.

Bryant, Bert. <u>Another Man's Life</u>. (unpub. m.s.) Alaska State
    Library. Juneau, Alaska. 1937.

Copeland, Carol Knight. <u>Always, Cathryne & Jess.</u> 1993.

Farnsworth, Captain. 1900-1902. Papers available University of
    Alaska Archives. Fairbanks, Alaska.

Foster, Helen. "Geology History of the Mertie Mountains."
    J.B.Mertie Mountain Dedication. Eagle Summit, Alaska.
    July 2, 1986.

Froelich, Arthur. Diaries: Mining on Seventymile River 1902-1916.
    Eagle Historical Society Archives. Eagle City, Alaska.

Graham, 1st. Lt. Harry. 22nd Infantry. "Military Historical Sketch of Fort Egbert, Alaska. Garrison School for Officers. Department of Columbia. March 1909.

Hall, Edwin S., Jr. "Aboriginal Occupations of the Charley River and Adjacent Yukon River Drainage, East-Central Alaska." State University College, Brockport, New York. March 1975.

McGregor, George. Diary 1919-1943. Eagle Historical Society Archives, Eagle City, Alaska.

Monroe, Father. "St. Francis Xavier Mission and Hospital, Eagle. August 1899-1904." Catholic Church Office, Anchorage, Alaska.

Pahlke, Loren. <u>On Two Frontiers: White Social Structure in Alaska Bush.</u> PhD thesis. Ann Arbor, Michigan. 1985.

Presbyterian Church. <u>History of the Yukon Presbyteria 1897-1974.</u> Anchorage, Alaska.

Reynolds, Arthur D. & Sadie. Diaries 1903-1945. (Nation River, Sam Creek and Fairbanks.) Eagle Historical Society Archives. Eagle City, Alaska.

Scott, Elva R. <u>Annual Roster Eagle Residents 1897-present.</u> Private collection, Eagle City, Alaska.

Wickersham, James. Diaries available Alaska State Library. Juneau, Alaska.